NOT LO

NOT
LOST

A STORY ABOUT LEAVING HOME

SARAH MARIA GRIFFIN

NEW ISLAND

NOT LOST
First published 2013
by New Island
2 Brookside
Dundrum Road
Dublin 14
www.newisland.ie

PRINT ISBN: 978-1-84840-302-4
EPUB ISBN: 978-1-84840-303-1
MOBI ISBN: 978-1-84840-304-8

British Library Cataloguing Data. A CIP catalogue record for this
book is available from the British Library.

Typeset by JVR Creative India.
Cover design by Nina Lyons.
Printed by Bell & Bain Ltd, Glasgow

New Island received financial assistance from
The Arts Council (An Comhairle Ealaíon), Dublin, Ireland.

10 9 8 7 6 5 4 3 2 1

For Ceri – without whom there would be no adventure and no book. You're, like, the coolest person I ever met. Thank you for taking me with you.

'There's a whole world off this island. It just takes one long swim to get there. Tell my mother I love her.'

– Joey Comeau, *A Softer World 18: Go, Emily, Go!*

Contents

Acknowledgements

Because this book is mostly true (except the parts that are tremendous, blatant lies) the people who appear in it, even for a moment, are all real. Tenderest thanks to all of you who agreed to let me tell the stories you appeared in. You were a terrific ensemble. You make being a grown-up way more fun than I could ask for.

Cast (In No Particular Order)

Ceri Bevan	as	CB
Evan Karp	as	The Scarecrow
Matthew DeCoster	as	The Tin Man
S.B. Stokes	as	The Sweetest Lion
Erin Fornoff	as	The Oracle
Ria Flom	as	The Only One Who Said Don't Look Back
Helena Egri	as	The Ruby Slippers
Patricia Kiernan	as	The Sea
Sean Griffin	as	The Sky
Katie Griffin	as	The Moon
Christina Duff	as	Evelyn

Damon Blake	as	*The Imaginary Friend*
Tom Rowley	as	*The Bard*
Gráinne Clear	as	*The Sound of Glasses Clinking on Dawson Street*
Dave Rudden	as	*The Destroyer of Worlds*
Belinda McKeon	as	*Wisdom*
Jenn Rugolo	as	*The Warrior Woman*
Jess O'Connor	as	*The Sound of Home*
Stephen Doyle	as	*The Best Whiskey*
Dee McKernan	as	*The Silversmith*
Deirdre Sullivan	as	*The Earth*
Matt Cahart	as	*The Noblest Heart*
Wonder Dave	as	*The Plainest in All the Land*
Des Bridgette	as	*The Best Denim Jacket in Donaghmede*
Tadhg O'Sullivan	as	*The Friendliest Face for Miles*
Kathleen Hale	as	*The Breath of Fresh Air*
Kerrie O'Brien	as	*The Composer (as He Steps into Fire)*
Amanda Simpson	as	*The Light Refracted*
Nate Waggoner	as	*The Absolute Worst Person in the World*
Sam Sax	as	*A String of Pearls*
Tatyana Brown	as	*A Venti Iced Sea-Salt Caramel Mocha*
Michelle Fang	as	*Moriarty's Gaurdian*
Sara Nelson	as	*The Only Sane One There*
Jamie Lundy	as	*The First to Say Hello*
Steo Fagan	as	*The Artist Formerly Known as Prince*
Cathy Boylan	as	*The Smell of Sea Air at Dawn after a Bottle of Wine*
Bob Birrell	as	*The Smoking Box in Front of the Atrium*

Lisa Keegan	as	The Skull in My Back
L.J. Quirk	as	The Pear Fairy Cakes in Your Mother's Bed
Laura O'Reilly	as	The Heart
Caitlin O'Mahony	as	Queen of the Netherlands
Catherina Behan	as	The Faraway Star
Natalie Woods	as	The Best Laughs I Had in Six Years of Schooling
Stephanie O'Toole	as	The Topshop Christmas Sale
Louise Mooney	as	Jim Morrison
Sheila Kiernan	as	Judy Garland
Paula Kiernan	as	Julie Andrews
Diarmuid O'Brien	as	The Badger
Zoe D. Tuck	as	The Quietest Encouragement
Rioghnach Ní Ghrioghair	as	Betty Draper
Baruch Porras-Hernandez	as	The Stage
Tim Toaster Henderson	as	The Enchanted Conch
Adrian Todd Zuniga	as	The Instigator
Pierpaolo Abbatiello	as	The Fellow Traveller
Ciaran Spencer Barter	as	The Dearest Old Friend
Alia Volz	as	The Hostess with the Mostess
Kevin Hunsanger	as	The Keeper of the Sweetest Rabbits
Katie Porter	as	The Sprigs of Lavender on The Altar
Roe McDermott	as	The Woman at the Front Line
Lauren Boyle	as	The Girl down the Road
Ian Keegan	as	The Friend of a Friend You Always, Always Bump Into

and

Moriarty Shitebag Casablanca as The Cat

This book would not have existed if it had not been for the support and belief and hard work of Vanessa O'Loughlin, Eoin Purcell and all at New Island. Thank you for everything. I still kind of can't believe it.

Thanks to Justin Corfield and Emma Dunne for their tender, clear edits, for pulling sense out of broken paragraphs and for being patient and encouraging. It means a lot.

I would also like to extend warm thanks to Ciara Kenny, Yalie Kamara, Anna Kemmer, James Kiernan, Rebecca Ford (for pieces of a nest), Colm Keegan, The Leporines, all at Quiet Lightning, Nic Alea (for Friday afternoons, for all of spring, for everything), Blythe Baldwin (for soda bread and crystals), 826 Valencia, Orla Tinsley, Joey Comeau for the epigraph, Dave Eggers for the chat and the advice, and Rebecca Gimblett: this book is titled after the tattoo on your wrist. Thanks to everyone who had me come and read on their stage or at their venue in the last year (bonus shiny hearts to the Booksmith) and who published things I wrote. Thank you everyone who has rooted for me, who rooted for this. It takes a village to build something that looks like this. There are so many people whose tenderness contributed to the composition and completion of this book. You know who you are.

Last of all, thank you, Ceri. I will never stop being grateful for you. You're, like, almost as amazing as Beyoncé. I love you.

Preface

So, here is a list of some things you should know before we start:

- This is not a book in which there is any great tragedy. I assume people expect tragedy from a memoir. There is none here. Something terrible almost happens in the autumn section. Almost.
- Most of this book is true. The bits that aren't true are very obviously outrageous lies. All of the dialogue is recalled from memory, so some of it is kind of made up. I do my best to be a reliable narrator – look, just come with me. It'll be fine.
- This is a book about a single year. May to May. I moved from my home in Dublin, Ireland, to a new home in San Francisco, California. I'm a statistic, really. Another postgrad who left because there wasn't enough work, who left because there was some weird, potentially fictitious promise of work and security elsewhere, who left because, well, adventure, I suppose. That's why a lot of us leave, isn't it? I arrived in America on the first of May 2012; I received the first contract for this book on the first of May 2013. It is a book about a year. It does not presume to be about anything other than that, I promise.

- When I was a teenage girl I loved relentlessly and without critique. This is when I started writing. I loved everything about every boy, every girl, every experience, wholly forgave awfulness and missing parts and cruelty because love then was all-consuming. It was fifty violins in a major crescendo, it was the crest of a wave, all day, all night, all the cells in my gawky body. Now I can love better, I can love with critique, with curiosity, with argument – dear God, I love an argument. I have grown-up eyes now and I like them. They are still capable of wonder, but also now able to question. This is why I talk like I do about San Francisco and Dublin. Such flawed, strange worlds, but still, so shiny, so beautiful, both. I don't like looking at perfection – I like running my hands through the guts of things, the guts of places, all imperfection. All chaos, some sapphires, some needles, all stories.

- There are two principal characters: me and CB. We're both in our mid-twenties. Usually protagonists are moderately attractive, but still relatable looking – crooked and ordinary enough to remind you of a cousin or an old boyfriend or someone you sat beside in Geography for six years but never really spoke to, while somehow still being handsome or pretty or cute enough to keep your attention through an entire journey. Imagine us as those half-strangers. There are photos of us in here somewhere too.

- As the book progresses more people, and a black-and-white cat, arrive and become part of the story, as they became part of our lives. I don't always explain where these people came from as they appear. When I found my feet, I threw myself into the literary community in San Francisco, because writing is what I always wanted to do when I grew up. I am a reluctant grown-up now, so I figured I had better pursue it now, or else it would disappear at the hands the fresh responsibilities that have cropped up everywhere these last few years. So, once I got the courage to step out alone, I attended readings and poetry slams in bookstores, speakeasies, sex shops, barber shops, bars upon bars upon bars – I met other writers and new friends by the dozen. Myself and CB started volunteering at a reading series called Quiet Lighting, and at the first show we attended we met almost all the people who would be our dearest friends and guides through this new city. This is where all the other characters come from, the audiences or stages of places where people go to read things to one another.

- I keep every business card that is handed to me, just in case. One was handed to me in Dublin back in 2010, and it was the butterfly wing that caused the hurricane, the storm of new friendships I was to gain in 2013. It was the key to the house, it is the first character in this book, that business card. (Thanks, Adrian.)

- So I used to write poems, a lot of them. I wrote them to figure things out and to connect to other people. But the way I look at the world now, as a result of living in America, brought about thoughts and ideas that were too big for me to fit into poems. America is much, much harder to figure out than anything I had experienced before. Poems got fatter on the page, and I realized I had started writing essays. Letters I knew I'd never send. Lists. Confessions. Scenes. Notes. Lies about raccoons. I couldn't stop writing these new things.

- At some point one of the weird things I wrote, due to somewhere between hard work and remarkable luck, ended up on the cover of *The Irish Times*. This was an essay about me crying in public due to hay fever, which transformed into being homesick, but then kind of getting over myself and moving on. That essay was the first murmuring of this book.

- I am not sure how I feel about the word 'memoir'. It feels like a word that is used for the work of people who have achieved a lot, who have been through wars, seen great sights, discovered things, survived things, made music, changed the world. This book really isn't a memoir because I am not one of those people. This is a book about a single year in which I did something that many, many people just like me do every single day. I left home. So memoir is not what this thing is. It is just a true story. Except for the parts that are enormous, staggering lies.

- Because I am a young person writing about being an emigrant, older people often ask me (with a smug, wannabe-private-investigator glint in their eye and the number of homeland security already potentially dialled into their phones) if I am here legally. Yes, I am (sorry if that makes me less exciting). My first visa was a postgraduate twelve-month internship visa; my current one is an extension of CB's employment visa. These are really boring details, but I am including them because you'd be surprised how quick people are to try and get other people deported.

- Look, every emigrant's experience is different. Hundreds of thousands of us have fled Ireland in the last few years. I can only tell you how it has been for me so far (it has been really weird). I am comforted constantly by the knowledge that many people have taken this journey in the past. Many are starting it right now. Still more will take flight tomorrow. We're all so different, but we're all together, too.

- I have had safe passage to America. I have learned a lot about what it means to be an Irish person here – or, to be more frank, a white person. Whiteness means a lot for an immigrant in this country: it means invisibility. Nobody has ever stopped me in the street to ask for my visa or my proof of residency; no security guard has ever followed me around a store suspiciously. There are hundreds of thousands of people for whom moving to America has not been as more-or-less smooth as it has been for me. I have been extremely fortunate. I pay close attention to this, and I am still trying to figure out what it means, how to place myself in the context of immigration here. I am still learning.

• I didn't wait thirty years to write this book, because by then this story would be so rose-tinted with nostalgia that it wouldn't be true at all. That tint of imagined tenderness is present when I write about Ireland because I can't help it: all this distance brings out fondness in me. Faraway mountains behind you look more gorgeous when you stop to look back over them than they did when you were dragging yourself up their cliffs. I didn't want the first year of living here to become that – all 'wasn't it great', when in reality it was 'Jesus Christ, this is so hard and so strange'. I needed to write it now, while it was close to me, while it was immediate and real. I did my best to capture it as it was happening. I took over two thousand photographs, you know. Really. I am still figuring a lot of things out.

What else? Oh, just a few last bits:

• There was way more swearing in real life than there is in this book.
• While I was writing the book I acquired two repetitive strain injuries, a two-week toothache and thirty-four mosquito bites exclusively on my feet. If you squint,

you can tell by the sentence structure what I wrote while I was in pain. Once, the cat stood on the Off button of my second-hand 2008 Mac Notebook and I lost an entire day's work and rewrote it really, really angrily. If you can guess what part of the book that is and tell me in person, I'll buy you a pint.

- This is just a story about leaving home. I am not an authority on anything other than doing my best and hoping for the best.
- My name is Sarah. I am twenty-five. I have green eyes and am left-handed.
- I have a little sister who turned eighteen and graduated from school and got her Leaving Cert results and had her debs and started college while I was gone, and that is something I think about every day.

Look, I just need you to know, if I didn't write this book now, I'd forget what all this felt like and I think that would be the real tragedy, forgetting. Imagine forgetting all this love and all this terror. All this growing up.

Introduction

*A*s you stand in the chaos of his going-away party, a girl with blonde curls turns to you with wet eyes and tells you that everything is going to change, starting now. She's right. You're leaving her behind soon. Your boyfriend is leaving Dublin in three days, and you are following him in six weeks. Neither of you has ever been to San Francisco before, but it is where you are going to seek your fortune, to try and build a new life. The moment Christina says this and throws her arms around you in the basement on Mountjoy Square will replay itself over and over in your head as the weeks count down to your departure. You will miss her more than you think.

The morning your boyfriend leaves, his parents will collect you both from Holles Street at four. It will rain, and nobody will say a word in the car, but your knuckles will be white from clutching his hand. He is going first, alone. You would give a limb, a pound of flesh, your two front teeth, to be walking through that gate with him, but you can't – instead you'll hold each other in Terminal 2 and smile and say see you soon, see you soon, pretending neither of you is crying. You will not tell him, even then, that you have the engagement ring already and that you will ask him to marry you in six months' time. The words are in your mouth, but you don't say them – you'll wait, and you'll be glad you did.

Above you both as you embrace is a huge painting of a stallion, mid-gallop. You laugh into his shoulder about its intrusion – the awkwardness of it, this huge horse looking out over your tender moment. You wonder how many people this creature has watched walk away from Ireland – how many goodbyes just like this one. You wonder what you will feel when the morning comes when it watches you leave. How soon that is.

You will move back in to your family home in the suburbs, away from your little flat near Holles Street. You will walk the coast every night, even when it is raining, looking out onto the industrial estates and Bull Island. It is late spring; it is raining a lot. Each night you will do the circuit faster until you are confident enough to run. You will run from your doorstep out into the evening, down the streets you grew up on, out into the village and then down to the sea. The air will be cold and wet, but you will move fast until you cut up to the Kilbarrack Road, all lit amber against the black. Even when you turn back towards your street, each footstep is taking you farther from home.

You won't answer your phone as much as you used to: when it rings you won't even look to see whose name has appeared. You'll spend evenings sitting on your sister's bed, laughing with her but wondering quietly how quickly she will turn from a teenager into a grown-up while you are gone. You'll find yourself hugging your mother more, finding excuses to hitch a ride into town with your father when he is going to work in the morning just for the half hour of his company, even if you're both too sleepy to talk. Sometimes you'll cut your evening walk short to sit with your best friend in her apartment on the Howth Road drinking tea until you're jittery. She'll quietly ask you not to leave, not meaning it. You'll tell her it's fine, you're not worried about losing touch, not meaning it either. She is leaving soon too – you are both chasing dreams you carved together ten years before. Let's make art and change the world, you promised each other. You would read stories down the phone to her from the stairs in your house, and Helena would paint pictures on the other end of the line. You would exchange them quietly in school, all teenage ambition, hoping that some day together you would build something great. There wasn't any notion in your teenage head that you'd be doing it five thousand miles apart.

The gatherings you go to to say goodbyes pass in a blur. You'll stay in touch, won't you? We'll always have the internet, won't we? Eight hours isn't that much of a difference, is it? So many people are gone already – you have been on the other end of these conversations more times than you can count. London, Japan, Holland, New Zealand, Australia, New York, Brazil – they've swallowed up almost everyone you know, and those who are left will nod over their pints and say, sure we'll be out the door after you in a few months. Most of them will go; some will hang on, playing violins on deck as the ship sinks.

You'll be warned about what to look out for by Erin, from North Carolina, who has lived in Dublin for two years. She'll sit on the winding stairs of the building she works in late one night, drinking a beer; honey drawl and bee-stung mouth, she'll tell you that when she first moved to Dublin she felt like everyone was lying to her. She'll lean against the wall and close her eyes, meaning this, this is advice; she'll tell you to find a new family, to ask everyone you meet to be your friend. That if she could do it, you could do it. You think how brave she is – you hope you can be that brave.

One night off Grafton Street, just outside Eddie Rocket's, Ria, who came from America around the same time as Erin, will tell you never to look back, to stay gone. And she'll smile because she believes you can do it. A drunk man will accost you both and comment that she is American – he will ask if you are too. He will ask if you are from San Francisco. You and Ria will laugh at how Dublin works sometimes, so intuitive. You will throw your hands up to the night sky.

The night before you leave will pass in a haze; you will be exhausted by the very idea that you're getting on a plane at dawn. Your aunts, uncles, cousins will pass through the house. Your grandmother, when she is leaving, will grip your hands tightly and her eyes will be sad. She brought you up: she is your hero. You promise her you'll talk to her through the internet in a few days – that she'll see your face soon. You'll offer to walk her to her house, thirteen houses up the road. She'll say no, that she's fine. You'll stand at the door until she's out of sight.

You won't sleep that night – instead lie awake in your now barren teenage bedroom. All the posters are long gone, the wardrobe organized neatly as storage space. When your father comes in to wake you, you will already be dressed. You won't remember the car journey, what was on the radio or what was said as you go up the Tonlegee Road and out over Donaghmede and the ghost estates of Clongriffin to the motorway. Your father fusses over luggage; your mother makes sure you're warm enough. Your sleepy-eyed sister hovers and keeps pushing tears from her eyes. You wear your grandfather's cardigan, striped with brown wooden duffels to keep it closed. You don't cry – instead point to the horse on the wall by the gates and laugh. There he is again, the absolute state of him, he's been waiting for you. All four of you knit close in a hug like none that has ever happened before, and you walk away to the slow line of people that leads to the security gates.

Everything is going to change, she said in the heat of the basement dance floor, and you took her in the crook of your arm and believed her. But you couldn't know, not ever, how huge that change would be.

Your family stay and watch as you pace the slowly dwindling queue. You still cannot cry. Your sister is making faces at you; your parents are waving. You reach the gate and disappear – you don't look back again.

Summer

This was what I'd wanted though – wasn't it? This
[wa]s the big, bold adventure I'd been dreaming of for us,
[th]at we'd somehow conjured into existence. This was it –
[thi]s was supposed to be fun, right? There was a constant
[ten]sion between moments of wild awe and adoration at
[the] tender beauty of the city and the hills, and the utter
[and] total shock of it, the alone of it. The confusion was
[ove]rwhelming, and I'd no idea how to beat it.

So I'd put on the headphones I'd bought in
[Dub]lin Airport and a big pair of Penneys sunglasses
[to] walk. I'd set myself miniature quests: a lifetime
[play]ing videogames taught me that the best way to
[make] a scary situation fun is to view it as something
[to] overcome and defeated – something that would
[make] me the hero of the day. My first quest was to
[find] a hairdryer. I have a long and sordid history of
[dram]atically damaging my hair with bleach, so I had
[to ta]ke care of the crunchy scarecrow mop I landed
[of]f with, and even a couple of days letting it air-dry
[ca]using me to leave a ginger trail of snapped split
[ends] everywhere I went. So, I decided the hairdryer
[woul]d be my holy grail, my princess in the dragon's
[keep,] the golden triangle I'd been destined to possess.
[I l]ooked up where one could acquire such a
[roy]al artefact on my fancy new internet phone –
[Hit]*chhiker's Guide to the Galaxy* – and followed the
[little] blue dot that marked my position to the tiny
[one] that marked my goal. Into the Mission I went,
[my] very first time – streets that I have since fallen
[comp]licated kind of love with.

All This Is True (I Think)

I would like to tell you that I remember everything about the first few weeks. I don't – I can only paste together flashes of the time as it was, even though it was only just a year ago. There was so much happening all at once, and so much nothing happening at all, that it is sometimes hard to say what happened during those first summer months. They are now a blur of tall, un-walkable hills, CB's hands after so long apart, strange discomfort at the new climate. They are a quiet memory. There were so many silent days in the empty new apartment. When I arrived all it contained was a too-small red sofa, an empty refrigerator, a table, four chairs, seven books and CB's clothes. The rest of it was untouched, wooden floored and blank white walled. I'd have settled for hideous wallpaper or ancient carpet. Something to prove that anyone had lived here before, that something had happened in this house before. But there was nothing, just quiet.

Now, a year later, it has a hatstand and a French scientific diagram of a Tyrannosaurus Rex from a science classroom and a globe and candles and a coffee table and a yellow chair from the 1970s and a real live sixteen-month-old cat – that is to say that now it is a louder place. It is better now, feels like us now. Back then it was not like us; it wasn't like anything at all.

CB would leave in the mornings when I would still be jet-lagged, glued horizontal, and he would stay at his job out in the wilds of Menlo Park until six or seven. Until then it was just me, so I did not spend a great deal of time inside the new house. This emptiness and quietness was a stark contrast to the life I had just left behind. The sheer music of my tribe back home, their stories, their complications, their absolutely constant presence – our old little nook near the Grand Canal always held some trace of them. An empty wine bottle on the table, somebody's jacket forgotten, two cigarettes in the end of a box of a Marlboros. The debris of good nights was non-existent here in SF. We didn't even have a bottle-opener, let alone friends.

San Francisco is gorgeous – our flat positioned high up enough for a sweeping view, but low down enough to be walkable for someone used to flatness in their cities. I would just stand there on the step for a moment, looking out at the odd angle of the street, wondering which way to walk. You'd be surprised how much of a tailspin it is to have people driving the other side of the road all around you – how easily that turns your left into your right. I am left-handed and have always had some difficulty differentiating left from right anyway, much to the frustration of any taxi

driver, who has ever had the discomfort o presence in their car – so this backwar city landed me almost perpetually lost. in the absolutely wrong direction. This made me frustrated and cranky, coup for directions making me feel like a to

At this point I had not yet lear best to have minor social interaction directions or buying a bottle of wat approaching a fake Californian dra my natural 'lilt' or 'brogue'. Fake acce lifetime of being subliminally fed A and cinema gives you a vague ide West Coaster' should sound like. embarrassment and the occasiona drinking habits.

Oh my gaaad you're Iiiirish – combination of syllables in the observation that I was never look to order some breakfast or ask if right direction for Noe Valley.

I learned to stop asking for di made me feel threatened and dif people to speak to me like I particularly difficult because th were often the only real live have until evening came, whe read the phonebook in his f accent. He was the last music of the orchestra was five tho

I still have this game I play with San Francisco where I look up and open my eyes and it shows me something new. There is always some strange hill lurking just beyond the buildings in front of me, iced with paper houses and tall, slim trees. These views fill me with the happiness I'd been looking for – just for a moment, but it is enough.

Mission Street herself felt immediately to me like a younger, wilder cousin of Moore Street in Dublin. Same vegetable vendors, same bustling community, same feeling of authenticity: like this street is so occupied with its own business and goings on that it does not have a moment to look at you unless you're buying some avocados, a bag of potatoes, some shrimp, some fresh salsa. Same feeling of a million stories happening all around you at once, but they pass by in a current: that pulse is how this place stays alive.

The first time I walked down Mission Street I was overwhelmed: it went on forever. It was such a long, long street. Everything was written in Spanish and, my God, how ashamed I was that I didn't have two words of the language to stick together. There were huge, derelict cinemas with grand, ancient signs punctuating sets of blocks ahead of me – I felt like I was the only person for miles who had absolutely no idea where they were going. Moving blue dot on a digital map or none, there was so much happening around me that walking fast wasn't an option.

There are two BART stops on Mission Street: 24th and 16th. The BART is like the DART, only it's Bay Area instead of Dublin Area (I still find this really funny). My goal was some way up from 16th, out through the grid to the cusp of a different village, Protero. This is a walk that is essentially, from my doorstep, turn left and walk for thirty minutes, then turn right and walk for fifteen minutes. I know this now, with all the cockiness a year in a village like this will support. At the time, this walk took maybe three times that long, and by the time the first two hours were over I was panicking down the phone to CB.

'I have no idea where I am.'

'Is your map not working?'

'It is but I'm really confused and my legs hurt and there's like a million hills and I have never seen so many yoga studios in my life and –'

'Follow the blue dot, you'll be fine, don't be scared.'

'But it's kind of raining and what if the rain gets in my phone when I'm looking at the map and then it's broken and then I have no map –'

'I believe in you.'

If he believed in me, I believed in me. Up Harrison, up Florida, onward south along 16th Street on a weird incline that made my calves pull but wasn't quite a hill, out amongst warehouses and empty parking-lots. There was a pet adoption centre, I noticed, promising myself to visit it some other time when I was not questing after the Magical Golden Hairdryer of Truth. I marked it on the map of San Francisco that I was slowly beginning to unlock in my head: things to do, places to see.

There, on the very top of the low hill at Protero, was my goal. Sally's Beauty Supply. I had read about this place on the blogs of glamorous young American women with beautiful tattoos who didn't appear to need any day job other than making handmade jewellery or handbags and standing in front of mirrors and taking pictures of their eye make-up. They shop exclusively in thrift stores. They collect statuettes of owls. I read a lot of these blogs, and my intake had dramatically increased in the lead up to moving to America. I had decided I wanted to become one of these stylish, offbeat young women once I reached my new home. I imagined myself with more interesting hair, more tattoos, a collection of ceramic forest animals of my very own, which I would take photographs of with vintage cameras (of which I would also have a collection), and impeccable personal style and make-up. Thousands of other young women would follow my blog, and I would make money from product placement and advertisements. How glamorous I would be, and it would all start here, at Sally's Beauty Supply, where I would purchase new make-up and colour for my fading hair, then I would take photographs of my purchases and blog about them and everything would start taking off! I would be a lifestyle blogger! With a stylish life to blog about!

Oh, Sally's Beauty Supply. This would be a Mecca of cheap professional hair-dye, exciting nail polish (I had never found nail polish exciting until this moment, but I was in America now, land of the expensive-looking seven-dollar manicure! I would do my own French tips! Maybe there would be glitter! Oh, imagine the blogs I would write about this!) and, most importantly, it housed the glory of the ancient necessity of womankind – the hairdryer.

By this stage in my travels it was raining very hard, but I wanted for nothing: rain on me all you want, San Francisco, I am going to buy a hairdryer and when I finally get home, whichever direction that is, I will dry my hair with it.

However, as I crossed the treacherous wilds of the vast and rumbling car park (read: parking lot, as I keep forgetting to call it), I was starting to become confused. There was a supermarket the size of a small airport, a Jamba Juice, a Starbucks, a pet supply shop, an OfficeMax – where was my beauty supply shop? Where was my Mecca of accoutrements and powders and bottles of peroxide? This was where my lifestyle blogging journey was about to start.

Of all the moments that have been lost and dissolved into the strange landscape of growing up that the last year has been, I will never forget this one. I just about launched into a fully fledged anxiety attack there amongst the gigantic American cars and shopping carts. I had come so far. I really, really needed a hairdryer.

Where. Was. Sally's. Beauty. Supply? I had been walking uphill for fifty years with hair made of icy sleet and only a fading blue dot to guide me. I had absolutely no idea how to get back to my apartment, and probably didn't have the physical strength to walk another fifty years anyway. I'd probably die of pneumonia and exhaustion along the trail somewhere, and CB would find my bones in a tiny heap outside the Goodwill on 19th Street.

I was not going to cry. I had not shed a single tear since I had arrived because I was a strong badass red-and-blue swallow migrating like it was no big deal, not a soft Irish child in a post-pubescent body – that is to say I was up to my eyeballs in denial. I was not going to cry in the car park. I was going to ask that security guard who looked like he could kick holes in mountains did he know if I was in the right place to find the Holy Blessed Golden Hairdryer of Triumph – or at least if, in actual fact, Sally's Beauty Supply was in the local vicinity.

After three or so minutes of 'Where's that accent from?' 'You a natural redhead?' 'I love Ireland – you guys love your potatoes, huh?' with me smiling not crying all the way through, he pointed his gigantic man-arm to the shadow of OfficeMax and there, like a mousehole in a mansion, was what I could only assume was the porch, or the reception area, of the grand palace of feminine decoration that I'd been questing after. I thanked the giant wholeheartedly and proceeded to the gateway to my goal.

Upon pushing the heavy glass doors open I was sure that I was about to enter a three-story escalator-filled palace, which would smell like dense perfumes and be full of mirrors and bright lights that immediately transformed my appearance from drowned pink-nosed rat to windswept heroine, but maybe the fifty-year walk had rendered me delirious. I did not expect, however, to land in what was essentially a glorified store-cupboard. Disappointment is a big feeling and a big word for something that should be as ordinary as discovering that a shop is smaller than you'd hoped it would be – but I was crushed. Everything in America was supposed to be bigger, better – where was the treasure cave I had somehow been promised by the American bloggers I aspired to be?

I slowly pottered down one of the three aisles in order to make them seem longer, hoping they sold hairdryers. Assuming they did. Bored now. Game over: I just wanted to crawl back under the duvet I'd woken up in, watch early nineties sitcoms on the internet and eat avocados with a spoon. I didn't even have the heart to browse – but, somehow, there on the shelf before me was something that made it all a little better.

The Thunderbird, a huge bright-yellow 1950s style hairdryer. Every time I wash my hair, to this day, I hold up the Thunderbird and tell myself this whole insane journey is going to be OK. It was the golden triangle I had been looking for. It was such a beautiful princess.

I have no idea how I made it home that day, only that I managed it alone and nearly certainly spent the rest of the evening in a heap under a duvet watching season one of *Friends*, eating Mexican food and relating really viscerally to Rachel's difficulty acclimatizing to life in New York. My blog went unwritten.

I swore to myself, however, that I would not get lost again. I would adventure slowly and with less reckless ambition: maybe stick to places on the obvious public transport grid for the moment, before toddling off into the wilds of the city limits. CB was sympathetic, and congratulated me on acquiring such a glorious treasure as the Thunderbird. I told him I could not promise that there would be no more frantic, terrified phonecalls – but that I would do my best.

The very next day I awoke refreshed, hungry again for adventure. Downtown! That is where I would go. It would be like Henry Street, or maybe even swishier, like Grafton Street. I would wander around until I found something useful for the apartment. Like some mugs! Yes, I would buy some mugs and maybe even two plates. I would eat lunch someplace like Bewley's and, oh, how I would marvel at the portion sizes and eat until my belly was sore! I would get the BART to get there, which was almost exactly like getting the DART – and on the way home, I would get the Muni, which is a streetcar, like the Luas, only it looked a little more like a set-piece from *Back to the Future*. How exciting! What a glorious day I would have! I had a shower and dried my hair with the Celestial Hairdryer of Glory and pottered off with a renewed sense of adventure. San Francisco was going to be my best pal on this bright, new day!

Downtown San Francisco is unremarkable. It is lodged between a number of gorgeous and fascinating districts, but I had not learned this yet. The mall is interesting because it is so locationless once you get inside. Everything else about SF has the facepaint of the culture all over it – hills, rainbow flags, townhouses – but the Westfield mall could be anywhere. If you squint your eyes hard enough, it could be Dundrum Town Centre. I still, to this day, sometimes spend afternoons just pottering around it, pretending I am not in San Francisco. It is air conditioned and smells kind of like caramel.

Visiting Downtown for the first time really solidified my distance from home in a way: the consumer culture so unlike Dublin, the shop assistants so aggressive, asking me what I used to dye my hair, asking me how my day was, asking me where I was from, asking all this of me when all I wanted was to walk around and look at things.

When I was younger, I'd fancied Americans the least stylish people in the world. Their clothes on television were ridiculous – this, admittedly wrong, attitude was probably due to the fact that my only exposure to them was nineties sitcoms. Oh, and tourists.

I worried, with no Penneys and no River Island, would I slowly become costumed as an American? This was the first time I realized that this experience would really change me. Even in a silly small way like how I dressed – it was going to make me different. The tools I had for constructing my identity in Ireland were different shapes now and would do different things. It was not going to be the same here – it was not going to leave me the same. I would hang America off my body until I looked just like it.

I didn't buy any mugs or plates that day. Eventually I just got on the streetcar back home. The L? It was the L, right? I had never been on one, so I had absolutely no idea I was going in the wrong direction until I'd been on it for thirty minutes and had to ask the lady next to me if this was going to Church Street: 'Oh no, honey, you're not from around here are you – where's that accent from?'

My phone was dead. The sun was setting. I got off at a station and realized quickly that the fog that I'd heard so much about was truly a giant ghost that would wrap its cold body around the hills so suddenly you never could see or feel it coming. It was the most frightening thing I'd ever seen, coupled with the empty roads in front of me, the slowly illuminating streetlamps and the black-screened useless phone in my hand. I had absolutely no idea where I was, only that I was at the end of the L line. The area around me was largely residential, but the roads were wide. I started walking, signs bearing street names that I'd never seen before not helping in the least.

I found myself walking uphill, unsurprisingly, which burned my legs and made my chest heavy. If I could have closed my eyes and clicked my heels three times at that moment, I would have. I was cold and anxious. I didn't even want to go to the new apartment; I wanted to be in Dublin, the little house on Hogan Place or the winding suburbs of Grange Park – I would have even settled for the wild student apartment I spent a year living in across from the Róisín Dubh in Galway. Anywhere but here. I was about to sit down on the path and take a little moment to myself to see if I could physically wish myself to somewhere I understood when I saw the sign, neon through the fog.

The Philosopher's Club. Gleaming at me in bright red – I moved towards it, relief rising in my gut. I walked inside: it was a sports bar, dark as a cave. Relatively empty but for a few middle-aged men in baseball caps sitting at the bar. I placed myself on a tall stool and placed my hands on the counter. The barman approached, asked what he could get me to drink. The floodgates, then, unfortunately opened.

'I emigrated here a week ago and am completely lost. Where am I? I need to get home. I have this little piece of paper with my address written on it. Can you call me a taxi? Do you have somewhere for me to plug this phone in? Also a charger? I'm very lost. What is this area called? I'm sorry. I'm sorry.'

The barman looked a little lost but then cracked a wide, Ted Danson, American smile.

'You Irish?'

'Yes.'

'You want a drink?'

'Yes.'

'You're in the West Portal.'

Where is that? I wanted to ask. Portal? What portal? Portal to the underworld? Portal to another dimension?

'Near Twin Peaks.'

My jaw all but fell off my face. Portal to a 1990s television drama it is, so. Twin Peaks, as in the haunted town populated entirely by FBI agents and serial killers? Twin Peaks, as in damn fine coffee and cherry pie? I didn't say anything, but stared at him, and assumed my eyes were screaming at him at top volume.

'Not that Twin Peaks. Where are you staying?'

'The Mission. Can I walk there from here?'

He laughed. 'Oh no, no no.'

'Do you have a number for a taxi?'

'Oh, there aren't many taxis around these parts.'

My gut sank, and for a moment I pictured George's Street at night, an ocean of yellow vacancy lights perched atop the thousands of taxis that pulse through Dublin's streets. Where were they now?

'But don't worry. We can call you a gypsy cab.'

I had no idea what this was, but I did not care.

'Yes, please.'

'And charge that phone.'

'Yes, please.'

'And a drink?'

'Yes, please.'

I felt like a small child as I sat there, nursing a beer. Like Paddington Bear with a note safety-pinned to his duffle coat. Negotiating this landscape was going to be full of moments like this, at the mercy of strangers.

Five hundred years later, the barman nodded at the door and told me the cab had arrived. He handed me my phone, charged, awake, and wished me good luck. I tipped him ten dollars for a three-dollar drink and all of his help and thanked him warmly. I did not know if the tipping thing was weird or not yet – I did not know how much I was meant to give, especially when someone helps you when you are upset and lost.

Outside in the thick fog there was a big white American car. I still feel childish for thinking this about all American cars, with the driver's seat in the wrong place and their broadness and newness. Jasmine was in the wrong-sided driver's seat. She had a soft smile. I sat next to her and took the little piece of paper out of my pocket. I did not pronounce Cesar Chavez correctly, but she understood where I needed to go. Dolores Street was the cross street, and this made me feel happy because it was my teenage-sweetheart's mother's name. She asked where I was from and I told her Ireland; she told me she's from Korea and has lived here five years. I asked her did she like it, and she told me she did: it is beautiful here.

We drove down big roads and I saw nothing but fog and glowing streetlamps. Beautiful? Hardly. Complicated and stressful and alienating and lonely, that sounded more accurate – but my sulking was cut short as we hit the top of a hill and began to decline. The whole of San Francisco opened up in front of me. It was golden and sparkling and not entirely different from the way Dublin city looks at a distance, out over

Bull Island when it's all just a line of orange fire in the night sky. The city was ablaze, and I could see a bridge leading out over the bay. It was so high that I gasped, and Jasmine laughed.

If this were a film she would have begun a monologue as we descended about how strange it is to be somewhere new for the first time, to be polluted with homesickness but infatuated like a teenager with the glory of a new city, of a culture and country that you know only from the movies. She would have told me her story, why she emigrated, if she was happy truly, if she ever missed her home. She would have given me advice, shared the secret of navigating a new grid, maybe handed me a map. When the lights rose above us instead of below us and we finally hit my new street corner, she might have taken my hand and wished me luck, but this was not a film and we didn't say anything at all. I wished her safe travels and she said thank you, and I closed the door to the big American car. I still have her card in my wallet, one year from then, when I know these streets better and have learned enough to share the secrets of this city with new immigrants myself.

As the weeks passed, I found myself getting lost an awful lot less, but feeling lost an awful lot more. I was not sure if that feeling would ever go away. Time began to speed up. Weeks dissolved.

This Is Why We Can't Have Nice Things or *Cat*

*W*hen his body moved back under the covers I started to wake up properly, having been in the strange half-sleep-space I'd taught myself to slip into when, months before, the cat had started to commence life-ruining in the hours before dawn. CB was sniffling, his body colder despite the enormous blue bathrobe he'd acquired at some point between our room and the kitchen.

I didn't think adopting a cat would mean this. I really didn't. Each morning between four and seven when the creature's slow, deliberate dismantling of our bedroom begins, I mumble an identical thanks to CB when he, soft touch, gives in to Moriarty first and rises to feed him. I know it well now, the rhythm of his walk to the kitchen, the creak of the press, the click and hiss of the tin opening, the scrape of a fork, the clink of the bowl on the floor, the padding of CB's feet back through the flat then back into bed. I cannot see anything during this time

– my eyes are still closed – but I know the melody of this daily routine so well that it becomes a part of my sleep.

This particular morning was during the phase where Moriarty had discovered the noise that our plastic, colourless, came-with-the-apartment blinds made. We don't have a window or balcony in our bedroom, just a strange set of ancient glass double doors and a steel grille, leading out onto a fire escape. The blinds look as though they belong in a clinic or a classroom from my childhood in the ashy grey of 1990s Ireland. That is to say, they are so ugly they cannot be disguised. They make a clacking noise when they move. They make a louder, more disturbing noise when they are the target of a certain small airborne feline's fearless assault.

This noise makes me think of bones being snapped, many bones all at once. It is a spine played like a tuneless xylophone. It is the warning rumble of the earthquakes that native San Franciscans keep warning me about. Clack-clack-clack, all foreboding and plastic. Sometimes it is the first sound I hear in the day – the overture to my new life.

I have almost learned how to tune it out – one morning the wind outside was wild and I focused so hard on the hush of the gale that the murder-clack just faded into nothing. Tiny victories. CB, however, has not mastered ignoring it. It gets inside his skin and he cannot rest until it stops. He faithfully, time and time again, rises to feed the creature, then returns sadly to bed, sleep broken, day begun far too early.

This particular morning, as he pulled back the covers and rejoined me, I leant into him tenderly, but he did not lie down to meet me. He was sitting upright, leaning forward. This alarmed me. I sat up to see what was wrong, still sleep-delirious.

His hand was clenched to his nose, bunched with tissues.

'Do you have a nosebleed?'

'Yes.'

'Are you OK?'

'Yes.'

'Did the cat give you a nosebleed?'

'I don't know. I don't think so.'

'When was the last time you had one?'

'I don't know.'

'I think the cat gave you a nosebleed.'

Nosebleeds freak me out because I've never had one in my life. They make me think of *The X-Files* and people having sudden, violent brain haemorrhages and alien capsules being implanted into the skin in your neck. I remember children having them in the playground and holding their heads back, nostrils crammed with toilet-paper, so that the blood rolled back into their system like nothing ever happened. I wonder where they are now, the nosebleed kids, and if they ever suffered repercussions as adults from all the runaway blood they drained back into their airways.

As CB sat there in the morning that came too early, head tilted forward, I was angrier at the cat than I ever had been. It was a bright, new, protective fury.

My partner was bleeding out of his face because of this creature. He had undergone what I still consider a violent psychic injury due to the disgraceful antics of an animal that had more fur than body mass. The stress and shock of the chaotic wake-up call had given him a gross science-fiction injury. I was so furious – why did we do this to ourselves, welcome this disaster into our home?

The cat entered our lives shortly after I first stepped onto Cesar Chavez with forty-eight kilos of my life in two cheap suitcases, jet-lagged and terrified. I had not expected the cold plateau of unemployment to follow me to America from home, and was finding it extremely difficult to connect with people – as a result, while CB was in work miles away in Silicon Valley, I was still wandering a lot on foot, trying to understand the language of San Francisco, hoping that if I put in enough footsteps it would suddenly all make sense to me. At first this habit was from necessity: I need to know where I am, so I'll go out into the world. It then grew into a ritual: walk to fill your day until something else comes along.

Every day I would wander a little further down into the grid of the Mission, picking up things in thrift stores to place in our hollow little flat that might make it look like home. My discomfort at being there had escalated to a seething hatred: this empty house was not what emigration was meant to look like. So I walked. The prettiness of the new city was enough of a distraction from the huge reality of what I had embarked upon with this journey.

This mapless wandering eventually took me to a huge set of buildings near a freeway bridge – they were familiar: I'd passed them before but had never yet been drawn inside. SFSPCA is a lot of letters, but I knew one of them stood for animals and I'm not sure what I was thinking, wandering in, saying I was minded to adopt a kitten and did they have any?

I have never owned a domestic animal in my life. Three kittens had orbited me throughout my adult life, at various distances. Cammy, a college boyfriend's Norwegian Forest cat with no eyelids. Lola, an old friend's pink-bellied tabby. Jaws, my former housemate's toothless black-and-white rescue. All made weird noises and were very small until they weren't, and were absent as soon as they grew out of this cuteness and became old enough to prowl suburban landscapes for baby birds to torture. Naïvely, I wasn't thinking that far ahead at all as I wandered the strange corridors full of snoozing, mewling balls of fur.

When I would hint, as a small child, to my father that kittens were lots of fun and a great idea, he would regale me with stories of the dead cats of his childhood: white baby ones found squished beneath packing cases in the garden, bags of them drowned in the Clonmel river, Mama and Fatso who lived and lived and bred and bred. 'Kittens turn into cats,' he'd say. 'Cats won't love you like you love them.'

Regardless of this echoing around my head, visiting the small creatures at the SFSPCA became a thing I did sometimes. This is not something I am proud of because, in retrospect, I honestly think it is a little bit sad. It is a clear reflection of how badly I needed company during those days – how completely disoriented I was. I'd turn the idea over and over that adopting a pet would be the thing that would plant me some roots in America. Maybe it would turn me into an adult – or, at very least, bring some reality into the barren, overpriced new home I found myself in. A thing with fur and lungs and eyes that needs to be fed and taken care of would bring normality, wouldn't it? People in the world swear they love their animals like brothers and sisters, don't they?

I entertained the notion of just showing up at the door of our flat with a kitten under my arm, but realized I had to have a conversation with CB before springing a life on him. I know this because, for our three-month anniversary, years before, I'd decided it would be romantic to bring him a goldfish. Here, new love of my life, is a goldfish in a jam jar that I brought all the way from a pet shop in Bray for you! It survived the whole journey on the bus even though the lad who sold it to me said he might not make it all the way to Christchurch but look at it go! Little fighter!

CB, having majored in philosophy in his undergrad, was not in the least bit impressed with this – a tiny life in a plastic bag was not a present. A life, Sarah. An actual life. I maintained it was not a tiny life: it was basically a plant with eyeballs. The existential crisis with gills, unnamed, lived for almost half a year. Most of that half a year it lived in a saucepan full of tap water. I like to think it lived a happy little fish life, floating in the blackness of the saucepan, almost a bit like drifting in space. In retrospect maybe we should have called it Astronaut, instead of nothing at all.

To avoid another saucepan situation, I said to CB that I figured a cat would ground us. Stop us running at the first sign of trouble. Plus kittens were adorable and possibly internet lucrative. We could be millionaires, CB, think about it: it's a business investment.

Whatever way that conversation went – through the inevitable 'Is this a practice baby?' moment, through the 'It's going to live for, like, ever: you know that, right?' sequence – it finally finished at 'Let's do it: this could be hilarious.'

I was very proud when I eventually returned to the SFSPCA with another person on my arm, because I'm sure the staff were a little wary of sad-girl-with-weird-accent-wandering-around-the-kennels.

Moriarty, then named Muffin, was in a puddle of his brothers in a 'kitty condo' with a television screen that played a loop of a flickering image of a forest bird on a branch. He had the longest hair of all of his siblings, was patched black and white like a tiny cow and looked a little like a reject puppet from the Henson Workshop, possibly around the *Labyrinth/Dark Crystal* era. I picked him up, and his fingertip-sized paw went straight for the emerald necklace I wore on my neck.

He was a thief. A bandit. Love at first looting – the little creep was coming home with us.

CB quickly revealed himself to be a kitten whisperer – the small thing would stand on his shoulder like a demented parrot on some sort of a glasses-wearing skinny-jeaned pirate. The kitten and I would lie in bed in the mornings when I scanned aimlessly through Craigslist writing/editing job listings. He was so small he could just lie on my sternum, purring like a handheld thunderstorm. I'd look over his little head and scan through the potential futures each listing held for me: I'd type up cover letter after cover letter and receive radio silence. I was still learning how to apply for jobs, still figuring out how to aggressively sell myself, and it was challenging. He didn't mind, though; he was there, constantly, reminding me I was not alone.

He, a little like myself, was poorly co-ordinated but had the ambition of a mountain climber. CB and I would invent endless histories for him, projecting a million stories onto him. He was a bank robber, a former punk rocker, a supermodel – he became a weird little catalyst for more sessions of hysterical laughter and elaborate fictional narratives than I ever had expected.

And yet, there he was that morning, sitting on the end of our bed, as CB bled out of his face. I was so angry, so enraged at that moment by how we hadn't had a full night's sleep since Moriarty came into our lives, so utterly and totally freaked out by the fact that my partner was bleeding profusely.

I held CB very tightly as Moriarty continued to ricochet himself around the bedroom, as he usually does at dawn, until we eventually passed into an uneasy last few hours of rest before we had to get up and be people, an unemployed intern and an internet detective.

When I woke up properly, later in the morning, CB having departed for Silicon Valley long before, the black-and-white creature was snoozing in a little ball beside me. I thought about the day ahead of me again: the strangeness of Americans and their television voices, how it was still so hard to connect with them. I scratched Moriarty under his chin; he purred, eyes blinking open all interstellar yellow. Maybe the new apartment wasn't so bad. Maybe things were going to be OK. A life-ruiner, sure. A holy terror. But absolutely a real, honest thing when California seemed anything but.

My Very First
Burrito or Hunger

*I*f San Francisco could eat itself with a spoon, it would. I mean that almost literally. There is a perpetual hunger here, some great tongue running around a hilly mouth, salivating fog, all while asking have you had brunch at that new place on 16th? There is a culture here, particularly in my neighbourhood, that treats food as though it were some holy thing. Some precious experience, some glamorous commodity. Organic, locally sourced, experimental, gluten free, vegan, dishes from all over the world in little nook restaurants and diners and trucks that pock the streets and are flocked to by lines of people, usually young people, often my age, but more stylishly dressed – though there is always a good flourish of real legitimate grown-ups too. They're all invested. They're all hungry.

Lines of people – or clusters, more accurately. I mean that literally. Often to get into a café or a diner, especially on weekends, it is well known that there can be up to an hour's wait. You sign your name on a list and stick around until it gets called. Outrageous? Yes. Who has time for that? My exact thoughts. Yet people wait. They chill out in the balmy sunshine complaining while staring into their smartphones, taking photos of their shoes or each other in their sunglasses. Like they've nothing better to do, standing in a seventy-person line outside Bi-Rite Creamery waiting for a ginger and lavender ice-cream sundae – like this is leisure, this waiting for deliciousness. They tell you with their calm, patient waiting that they are totally down with waiting for this double scoop, for that honey olive-oil ice-cream, for that balsamic strawberry delight, for an hour, a whole hour, because they treasure this scoop. This scoop means a lot to them.

I had never seen this in Dublin. Myself and CB had a regular place we'd go to for Sunday brunch (oh, how little we knew in those days of the great and masterful daytime episode that is brunch) in the docklands. Usually we'd be hungover or un-showered, often both. We'd crawl up to the modern, minimally designed, Ikea-looking restaurant and the waitress, blonde with shoes I always liked but was too shy to ask about, would lead us to our table and we'd have our eggs benedict and everything would be fine. Nip in, nip out. Some days, however, we'd arrive and there would be a couple or a family ahead of us, implying a wait. We would throw our hands up to the sky dramatically and pace off towards the Spar where we would bitterly purchase sausage rolls and chocolate croissants, pretending not to enjoy them, in spite. We would never wait. Never. Even if it was only going to be ten minutes and we had nothing planned for the rest of the day, it was an absolute nope if ever there was one.

Now, however, having opened the great pantry door of San Francisco, we have been utterly transformed. The lines outside restaurants absorb us; we stand around tapping our toes, making inane observations about the street we're standing on or seeing who can say the word 'TITS' the loudest without getting embarrassed, until we are granted entrance into these impeccably hip dining halls, these tiny pleasure domes.

So we've become them, those fools standing in line. And that's, well, assimilation, right? Emigrant learning curve: just giving in to the cultural movements of the city you're living in is OK. Even if some of them appear really stupid. Just because you wouldn't do it in Dublin doesn't mean you can't do it wherever you are now, right? Just because you can hear the ghost echoes of your former, pre-emigration self actively laughing at you and calling you a thick doesn't mean what you're doing now is embarrassing or ridiculous in any way. Even if it is wasting an hour of a perfectly good Saturday standing outside the same restaurant you ate in last Saturday. And the Saturday before. Don't be so hard on yourself. That's what people do here.

Restaurants and diners are cheap. Supermarkets are expensive. It costs more, or exactly the same, to make yourself a meal at home, especially if there's meat involved, than it does to eat out. Even the regular markets (the ones that aren't full of locally sourced, peach-fed poultry and hand-groomed apricots – of which there are many) – even the distant cousins of Tesco are shockingly expensive.

Besides, when you're starry-eyed and caught up in the whirlwind of a new city, who wants to eat at home? When your apartment literally doesn't have any pots, pans or utensils, why would you eat at home? When a plate of fresh food the size of a small village costs $7? When you have no job, no friends and your boyfriend is in Silicon Valley for ten hours out of every day, why in the name of God would you eat at home? When, in so much of the American media you've been fed, there's been an interesting protagonist with a casual rapport with a waitress in a local café. Especially writer types. Whenever they walk in the doors of said café the lovely waitress greets them by name and says, 'The usual?' And in my imagination, I say, 'Good morning, Thelma, thanks, the usual would be great.'

This scene does not easily come about. What meal would it be? Where? I have never done this before so I'm not sure how much attendance at a diner is creepy and how much is normal. CB and I were never remembered even once at our weekly haunt in the docklands in a whole year. Would it take a year? Two?

Who knows? It was just me and my mission. This would be my new quest. Achieve a 'The Usual'.

Eating alone is strange. It was a harsh, sudden new routine. Before CB and I left, I'd moved home to my family house and had been eating with them. During the day, I'd eat in the chaos of the staff room in Collinstown Community College with Rebecca, the tender-hearted librarian who was my collaborator in the modules I facilitated. If I wasn't in the school, someone would be at the kitchen table of the house drinking tea with me and eating soup. Even before I moved home and was still living in the little flat off Love Lane, there was always going to be somebody around with whom to scull tea and break bread. Everything changed then. There was nobody. Just me and the Mission.

And I began eating and nobody could stop me. I ate for my country, for my sanity; I ate all of my sadness and my celebration too. I ate everywhere that would feed me. I kept myself to around about a ten-dollar (plus tip) a day breakfast/brunch budget and still managed to experience a whole lot of what the city had to offer me. I started eating fruit for the first time in my life. I had previously been almost afraid of fruit, and its tendency to pillow with mould or brown after only a moment or two (apples are the most notorious perpetrator of this hideousness) usually kept me at a very strict arm's length. But this is assimilation again: how could I live in California without eating all the fruit?

They do fruit here that I had never seen in my life before. Cantaloupe and honeydew, new sweet melons became obsessions – how much honeydew can I eat, can I eat so much that I swell and become one, become a spherical green planet full of water and sugar? I think I can. Avocados, too.

Oh, avocados. They arrived into my life and immediately become the softest things I had ever known – I had a brief altercation with one once in the lush fruit and vegetable aisle of Fallon & Byrne on Wexford Street and paid something outrageous and sad like four euro for it because I was really curious about what it would taste like.

Rubber, I had thought, slicing awkwardly into it, no clue how to navigate its thick skin, its planet-like seed. I didn't like it. So I tried to wait for it to ripen. Here, little expensive avocado, do you want to live on the windowsill? The radiator? Here is a little Tupperware box for you to live in until you are ready to become what I have always dreamed you would be. I was like a mother hen coaxing an egg into a tiny chick. Where would it be most comfortable? Where could I sweet-talk it into the deliciousness I had predicted for it?

It went brown by the next morning. I swore off them then, and was uninterested in them from there on in, until San Francisco sprawled its sundae-with-sprinkles hills ahead of me and I noticed that they were everywhere. The markets that lined Mission Street were full of them. They were suddenly on burgers, a side order, on eggs. Oh Lord, were they ever on eggs. These weird little buttery pods were suddenly important, a staple. A symbol, maybe.

I decide that how my new diner, wherever it may be, will remember me is because I will order a side of avocado with everything. That will be my calling card. Genius.

Come June, Kerrie comes to visit me. She's buzzing around America touring her poetry book, and she's exactly the right size to sleep on my and CB's tiny sofa, so she lands in the Bay for a week. Kerrie has excellent posture, the driest wit in Ireland and extremely psychic tendencies. We met a long time ago, somehow, something to do with poetry readings, and continued to physically bump into each other in the street, at bars, week after week after week until we took the hint from the universe to just become friends. We think we're going to spend all week drinking, being cackling terrifying poet-women, more gin than salt in our bodies, but in actual fact we just eat. We walk around the city and we eat. She befriends tiny, mewling Moriarty, who is at this point only three months old and around the size of a potato with legs. He sleeps on the sofa beside her.

I am so grateful at this point for her presence that I have a hard time hiding it. I feel like I am less likely to go insane; like, for one week, I am grateful to be unemployed so I can dash around and be a tourist. CB goes to work early; I wake up, trundle into the kitchen and drink a cup of tea with Kerrie. We go to Chloe's, the corner breakfast joint on Church Street. Chloe's was started by a couple who used to do food catering in Hollywood and, after feeding the cast of *Dirty Dancing*, started Chloe's with the proceeds. We eat eggs and avocado. Kerrie cannot believe the avocado. Neither can I. We sing prayers to it.

We eat breakfast other days in Red Café, a Mexican joint. We sit at the counter and I eat plantains and avocado. Plantains are like bananas, only different and better. They're like the long-lost cousin of bananas that you deep fry and eat for breakfast. Kerrie eats fluffy pancakes with syrup. We talk a lot about poems and writing and what we want to do. I tell her I haven't been writing poetry lately, that everything just comes out longer, that it won't stay down the side of the page.

That evening she tells me I should read Anne Sexton, Moriarty in her lap. I attempt to cook, making a sort of successful chorizo and bean stew. Cooking has been hard for me – carrots don't taste right here and mushrooms are expensive and we still don't have any real utensils in the flat. But other people eating the food I make warms my heart in big, big ways. I make the stew with gnocchi as a base.

After we eat we find Anne Sexton poetry on the internet and read it to each other. My stomach hurts, but I tell her my stomach has been hurting a lot lately. Almost every day. Kerrie doesn't think that sounds good, that maybe I should keep a record of it. I think hard, knees at my chin on the red sofa. What has been giving me that sick feeling?

Bread. Croissants. That night we got deep-fried sweet-and-sour chicken balls. Pancakes. Gnocchi, now, on the list of offenders. Oh, beers too. Can't drink beer any more. I had a bagel that was pretty painful recently too. It was a strange feeling. Usually I had to lie down in a ball until it went away.

'What do they all have in common?' she asks. 'Maybe you have an intolerance or an allergy?'

It takes me a few minutes to realize that it is wheat.

Does this mean I have to give it up? Do I have to give up bread? I love bread. Bread is the best. I don't know what I'll eat without bread – everything has bread in it. I was never allergic to bread before, I tell her. Kerrie knows things about food because her ma's a WeightWatchers' leader. She says American wheat is different.

This hits me hard and I am dumbstruck. Am I allergic to America? To their French-toast cream-cheese strawberry sandwiches? To their towers of blueberry pancakes? To brownies? Blondies? Cupcakes? To their locally produced micro-brewery organic beers? To that weird sourdough bread that seems to come with everything? To the soft, velvety tortillas that burritos were nestled inside of? To cereal? To everything I like? There can't be gluten in avocado, can there?

I deal with this discovery much in the way that I deal with most things I don't like: I pretend it isn't happening for a while. I don't go to a doctor because

I don't have a doctor here; also I have watched documentaries about the American healthcare system and am afraid of owing seven thousand dollars to a general practitioner. I refuse to be allergic to America. This will not deter me.

Kerrie and I flit around the place with Scott. CB and I had met Scott at the first ever literary event we'd attended, and immediately became fast friends. He is tall with a beard and soft eyes; he wears a ring with a skull on it and has lived in the Bay Area for so long that it sometimes feels as though he keeps all of its stories. We drive over the Golden Gate Bridge out into the Marin headlands, which carry the feel of a different planet. We eat in In-N-Out Burger on the wharf – a legendary fast-food chain that I had heard tell of through vines of people, with its secret menus and perfect, fresh produce. I bit into my Double-Double Animal Style Cheeseburger knowing full well that the fluff of the bread would soon turn my stomach to pieces. I cared not.

The week had been joyous, but then she was gone. Back to eating alone. Back to figuring out this wheat thing, this emigration thing too. No more pretending I was on holiday. Back to my mission.

Four nights in a row I attempt to make boxty. Boxty is mashed potato, grated potato, flour (in my case, gluten-free flour-esque mix out of a bag) and egg whacked in a frying pan until it becomes an old Irish tradition. My family never ate them, but somewhere post our first trip to Bed, Bath and Beyond, when I had finally acquired some cheap pots and pans, I took it upon myself to begin a tradition: The Griffin Boxty.

The Griffin Boxty looks and smells like nobody survived the fire. It was meant to be somewhere between fluffy and crispy with cheeky garlic and spring-onion notes, but everything is consistently wrong. The stove heats up too fast. I keep forgetting what cups are to ounces. The blender makes everything like liquid. I feed CB the botched attempts. He eats them with a forced grin, bless his long-suffering heart, and I storm around in outrage. The cat keeps getting in my way. I pick him up with my potato hands and drop him on CB's lap. Cat hair everywhere. Cat hair boxty. Wash everything. Start again. Burn everything. Start again.

When in the kitchen I usually get furiously creative, something like I imagine Nigella Lawson would be after half an ounce of Purple Haze. I can breathe life into any basket of random groceries – Doctor Frankenstein has nothing on me. This is because I only learned to cook two years ago, so I still have all of the blind, indestructible courage of someone who's never made anything gross. There was only one incident in my brief and illustrious culinary career in which a kitchen was set on fire, and that was more the ancient cooker in CB's old flat on Patrick's Street than it was mine – everyone knows that, so I won't take the blame for it and, for the record, we still ate that pasta, and it was fucking great, thank you very much, so I'll hear no more about it.

It is, on night four of my refusal to stop trying to make edible boxty, tragically apparent that my previously assumed culinary precociousness was merely beginner's luck. My grandeur crumbled before me, like so many poorly constructed potato cakes. I have no idea how to cook boxty. It should be so simple, and yet every time it hits the pan it is a gross slop, a charred mess.

Not only am I allergic to America, but I can't even master the most basic of Irish traditional dishes. Everything is changing and I am really upset.

There's this café on the corner of Valencia and 22nd Street in a gutted old drug store. The façade is still there, all written-on ancient signage, DRUG STORE faded and peeling. The café is called Boogaloo, though that isn't written anywhere outside it. The inside has black leather booths, the walls a mosaic of broken dishes and local artists' work for sale. On a long shelf near the ceiling there are old records with various song and album titles incorporating the word Boogaloo. There are huge windows and you can see in, see everything from the street. Sometimes, on sunny days, there are tables and chairs outside. It is not a remarkable spot, visually; just a dive breakfast joint with attractive, well-dressed staff. They play really nice music, sometimes Sex Pistols, sometimes the Cardigans, sometimes Angelo Badelamenti's David Lynch movie scores.

One waitress, amongst the collage of tattoos on her arms, has a black linear image of a shark's fin protruding from minimal, cartoonish waves. 'DUH-NUH' is written above it. Like duh-nuh, duh-nuh, approaching terror from the deep music, like *Jaws*, like how clever, like I love her, even though she doesn't say much.

She is not the one who begins to remember me. Another curly haired, straight-teethed lady does. Then Johnny, then Amy, then Manny. It's because I can't eat the bread parts of what I order that they remember me. Corn tortillas instead of bread, please, and a side of avocado. I eat here maybe twice a week and, slowly, hellos of recognition chirp from the chorus of staff. Something starts happening, and I know the day will come soon when they ask that two-word question and I say, yes, thank you, my usual would be great. Great.

The very first day I arrived CB brought me a long cylindrical thing wrapped in tinfoil. It was piping hot, the length of my head, with a radius that probably wasn't far off that of my upper arm. This was the first burrito of a long, dangerous love affair.

Dublin arms itself with chicken fillet rolls and breakfast rolls – the long-lost cousin of the burrito. I'd attempted to eat one once, hammered at 4 a.m. on Wexford Street, and been furious. Beans? Rice? In a wrap? Piss off, I'm going for a three-in-one and a bag of prawn crackers – oh, how I rejected them vehemently, for no reason other than one less-than-delicious experience. This bad experience blossomed into a casual, 'Nah, I'm not really into Mexican food,' in conjunction with a lifelong, 'Nah, I'm not really into spicy food.' Basically all I ate was bread and soup and potatoes. Chicken fillet rolls. Breakfast rolls. For shame, my narrow-mindedness. For shame.

Essentially both the breakfast/chicken roll and the burrito are spawn of the sandwich. Portable, affordable, not especially nutritious but filling enough to carry you through the day (or night). Starchy enough to quell a drunken stupor or vicious hangover, convenient to eat swiftly when walking or commuting from one place to another. Not entirely messy, but not entirely neat. Street food, kind of, I suppose.

So, this I have learned. Tacos are like little burritos that are open instead of wrapped shut. Nachos are like pizza, only messier and better. Quesadillas are like cheese sandwiches (in fact there is little to no distinction between the two things, only that the cheese sandwiches I grew up with are square and quesadillas are circular and made with corn tortillas). Chilaquiles are eggs with corn chips crushed into them, served with really spicy sauce. Chimichangas are deep-fried burritos. Tortas are sandwiches. Mexican food is hearty, and everywhere in the Mission. I'm not even sure what I ate before it. Bread, I suppose. Things with wheat in them. The deliciousness of this new world of food made the grieving easier. Avocados too. They soothed me.

I put on weight. Like, a lot of weight. Weight that I don't recognize on my body in photographs. I look at pixellated scenes of myself standing at a microphone on

Bloomsday night, reading Molly Bloom's monologue from the bed, and have no idea who that person is or where the sharp jawline and jutting collarbones of my teens have gone.

Hitting your mid-twenties is funny like that. Nobody tells you your body is going to keep changing, that woman is as complicated as teenage girl, that there is no plateau of ease and maturity after puberty, that bodies are fluid and continue to grow and expand and contract and expand, and expand.

I join WeightWatchers. I sit in a room of other young women on Tuesday mornings, all on breaks from their South of Market high-flying jobs, who talk about their compulsive eating, talk about talking to their therapist about compulsive eating. We get stickers from the perky mid-thirties group leader for defeating our cravings. I do make one friend, a marine biologist and professional sailor. She has lots of cool stories and her eyes are yellow. That kind of makes the whole circus worthwhile. I drink a lot of diet sodas. I lose a stone. I put it back on again. I stop caring. Eventually, I don't go back.

America is under my skin now. I have eaten so much of it that I am swollen with it.

I have dreams about my mother's dinners. I am angry at my teenage self and her selective, anxious appetite for rejecting them night after night, for favouring quarter pounders with cheese from the Hamburger

Bar on the Kilbarrack Road over them. I miss the Hamburger Bar on the Kilbarrack Road. I miss our kitchen table, our dinky refrigerator, the constant presence of King Crisps and Cadbury snack-size chocolate bars. I miss my sister's insistence on leaving the teabag in the boiling mug until the water is black and bitter. Sometimes I imagine her chewing paper teabags just to get her hit. I miss how my nana would make batch-bread ham sandwiches and leave them on the kitchen table for me in a tiny wicker basket with a paper napkin inside it, although it has been years since that was a regular occurrence. I think about how perfect the stew she made was: the coddle. If I close my eyes I can see our pantry, the little plates of the teacakes my mam would put together. She'd slice the top part off and cut it into two semicircles, place a dab of cream on the exposed cake then replace the soft little half-moons like wings on top of what was then a fairy cake. They'd sit on saucers and dinner plates around the house, one by one disappearing.

I could order in King Crisps and Cadbury bars off the internet in bulk. I'm sure with a little wrinkled forehead concentration I could emulate a quarter pounder with cheese from the Kilbarrack Road (actually, to be fair, In-N-Out Burger blows it out of the water). Sandwiches are nothing special – I definitely saw mini-baskets in the little dollar store on Mission. Fairy cakes are, even for the mad scientist in me, a basic paint-by-numbers recipe. You can even get the mixture in a box, pre-made. I have so much Irish tea in this house I could start running a business (I packed several boxes and receive supplements in the post). I can't even eat most of these things now, and if presented with them would probably have to politely decline, or obnoxiously ask about their wheat-flour content, or discreetly pick the ham from the sandwich and eat it sticky-fingered and lean. Sometimes I wonder what has become of me.

When you can't taste things, do you forget them? How much is forgotten with that taste?

Hunger and homesickness are pretty much the same thing, right?

Look. None of this is about the food. Not really.

Twelve months from Kerrie's visit, from boxty-gate, from my first footsteps into Boogaloo, CB and I will be a roaring, laughing calamity of drunk one Saturday night. We will have rolled home from a dance party populated almost entirely by people in fur animal suits; we will have had late-night wine in Baruch and Dave's house with Sam there too – gosh, we will have friends by then. Good ones.

We will have picked up late-night burritos from El Faralito on 24th Street. They will be heavy and large and we will be starving; we wait all the walk home to eat them – our hunger will deepen with every step.

We will greet the hill we live on with battle-cries, clinking our bottles of Mexican Coke (made with real sugar instead of corn syrup) as we stride. When we hit the red sofa and begin to eat we will be silent until the crazy drunk hunger subsides a little, then we will start to talk.

'Do … do you remember, Charlie's? Charlie's three-in-ones? It's around that time of night,' CB will say.

'Ohmygod. Chocolate croissants out of Spar in the morning, please,' I will reply. My mouth will be full of avocado and rice.

'Do you remember the time Ho-Ho's gave you orange sauce instead of sweet and sour sauce with your chicken balls?' he will go.

'I nearly murdered someone that night, I swear to God. Ugh, give me a Queen of Tarts chocolate scone. Now.'

'A scone, Jesus. Oh, oh – DiFontaine's pizza. When Eamonn Doran's was still Doran's instead of whatever it is now. Madonna's? Was it Madonna's last time?' Neither of us is sure.

And we will talk and talk and laugh. Rick's Burgers. Yamamori. Simon's Place. Perogi from Uncle's in the Moore Street Mall. AHache, the Apache Pizza hatch on Bachelors Walk and the best pun in the universe. The deli counter in Fallon & Byrne. 3FE in the Twisted Pepper. Thousand House on Abbey Street (with a missing T so permanently reading 'Housand House').

We will eat our burritos and we will walk the topography of the places where we ate back home. Who was there, what was happening. We won't be hungry any more then. Not at all. We will be full.

Four Lies and a Truth or Let Me Tell You a Thing about Raccoons

S arah was beginning to get very tired of sitting by her sister on the bank, and of having nothing to do: once or twice she had peeped into the book her sister was reading, but it had no pictures or conversations in it, 'And what is the use of a book,' thought Sarah, 'without pictures or conversation?'

So she was considering in her own mind (as well as she could, for the hot day made her feel very sleepy and stupid), whether the pleasure of making a daisy-chain would be worth the trouble of getting up and picking the daisies, when suddenly a Raccoon with black eyes ran close by her.

There was nothing so very remarkable in that; nor did Sarah think it so very much out of the way to hear the Raccoon say to itself, 'Oh dear! Oh dear! I shall be late!' (when she thought it over afterwards, it occurred to her that she ought to have wondered at this, but at the time it all seemed quite natural); but when the Raccoon actually took a watch out of its *waistcoat-pocket, and looked at it, and then hurried on, Sarah started to her feet, for it flashed across her mind that she had never before seen a raccoon with either a waistcoat-pocket, or a watch to take out of it, and burning with curiosity, she ran across the field after it, and fortunately was just in time to see it pop down a large hole under the hedge.*

In another moment down went Sarah after it, never once considering how in the world she was to get out again.

Lifted affectionately from the opening pages of Lewis Carroll's *Alice in Wonderland*. Please read the Raccoon as it appears in the coming passages as a metaphor for a thing that would never happen in Ireland, could only happen in America. Read the appearances of the Raccoon as strangeness, as newness, as a sign that there is no going back. Read the Raccoon as truth in disguise. Read the Figure Skater as a lie intended to conceal the person in question's real identity.

I

When I see the raccoon I am lying on my belly on the living-room floor of a hundred-year-old house in the Inner Richmond district. I am holding a long plastic medicinal syringe in my hand and I am out of breath. I have been crawling on the floor for forty-five minutes and am so tired I could cry. I have bruises all over me. It is 8 a.m.

It is not the raccoon I am chasing, but rather a large white rabbit called the Yeti. He is a six-year-old lion-head rabbit with a tumour in his neck the size of a hardboiled egg. I am bunny-sitting him and his sister, Roscoe, for three days. He has cancer real bad. I didn't even know rabbits could get cancer, but there you have it.

For a terminally ill domestic animal around as big as a handbag, he can still run pretty fast, and is in no way interested in allowing me to catch him and feed him the syringe full of drugs that will keep him alive.

I am cold at this point because I have no idea where the central heating is located and don't feel right snooping. The hardwood of the floor is icy; this district is the coldest of the fourteen microclimates in the Bay. I have just panicked down the phone to CB that I cannot catch this rabbit and what if he dies and what if I have his innocent blood on my hands because I wasn't fast enough to catch him and his awful little sister is just encouraging him to hide from me – they're conspiring, I told him, conspiring. CB finds this hugely entertaining.

I am Elmer Fudd in a nurse's uniform, armed with medication instead of a gun. I am so afraid I'll never catch this Yeti, this absurd white, dying rabbit. His owners, Alia and Kevin, are a writer and a bookstore owner. I desperately want them to think I am a copped on, cool person.

I do not know enough people in San Francisco to casually go around murdering people's pets and expect it not to ruin my life as well as theirs. When I finally swoop in on the soft, fast, sick little animal, I hold him under my arm with his legs pressed tightly to my side just as Kevin had showed me, so that even if Yeti tries to kick himself free he won't break his own back in the process.

In the kitchen I place him on the table, on a white towel. I place the syringe into his little mouth: it clicks against his teeth. He greedily eats the contents as I press down the injection of it, as if remembering after all the wildness of the chase that he needs this to live. He is a gorgeous thing, snowy grey and soft.

When we are done I bring him back to his sister, a black mirror image of him, and they scamper off together under a table. I leave them a little mountain of banana chips as thanks for permitting me to keep Yeti alive. I collapse onto the stylish 1970s sofa and put my face in my hands. I am so cold. Is it too early to text Alia and Kevin on their vacation to ask about heating? It is not even nine yet. It is too early. I wish I knew where the central heating was. I hope this rabbit doesn't die.

As I lift my head up I notice the raccoon. He is eating the banana chips with his little hands. He pauses and our eyes meet, a tiny yellow crisp suspended halfway to his mouth. Yeti and Roscoe are staring at him, huddled close now under the coffee table. The raccoon drops the chip and it clacks quietly against the wooden floor. I blink and he is gone. Yeti and Roscoe do not move a muscle.

Months later I will learn that Yeti died at home, with Alia and Kevin holding him. I will read Alia's status update on the internet and there will be tears in my eyes, both of sadness and relief. He was a good creature.

II

I am sitting at a table in a bar in Oakland, two glasses of wine and four pints of water into a conversation that I don't have the emotional skills to shut down, when I see the raccoon. So this professional figure skater has invited me out for drinks and conversation about my craft, and who am I to say no to a glass of Pinot Grigio and a jar of pickled vegetables the size of my head, coupled with a real legitimate grown-up professional figure skater who actually wants to talk to me about the work I'm trying to make? Boozy conversations about poetry with professional figure skaters? This is in my top five favourite ways to spend an evening, squeezed between eating Chinese takeaway while playing video games on the sofa and sweaty dance marathons at warehouse raves.

Unfortunately I had not anticipated the professional figure skater's hand to creep somehow across the table to mine and him to calmly ask me in a measured tone if I would have an affair with him. There is a paler ring of skin where his wedding ring must usually live, except on evenings like this. His skin is pink and dry. He is older than my father. He has more accolades than anyone I have ever met. I see the hundreds of young girl figure skaters who have fallen for this. I move my hand away and reach for my wine.

In retrospect, I probably should have seen this coming. This bar-in-Oakland scene is our second encounter, and our first should have been a dead giveaway for that hand creep, that awful suggestion. Our first encounter had been at a figure-skating event at Golden Gate Park, where he was skating and I was volunteering. A mutual friend had introduced us and we'd clicked: he'd taught a few figure skaters I knew in Ireland and, oh, isn't the world so small, la de dah, usual small talk, oh, how long have you been here, how long are you staying?

It is important to here note that somewhere along the line he had misinterpreted CB's first name as a woman's name, which is an extremely common mistake for people to make, due to the fact that CB's first name is actually, in basically every country that isn't Wales, a woman's name. In fact in Ireland it's a pretty common woman's name. So the professional figure skater really couldn't be blamed for making that mistake. The following mistake, however, I'm not so sure.

He asked me was I planning on staying in America for good. I told him no, certainly not, I wanted to move with CB to London, where many of our friends are either based or heading towards when their own adventures are through. I also admitted that I wasn't really keen on settling down in America, wasn't really into the idea of having children so far from our families.

The professional figure skater recoiled from this in shock. 'Really? Kids?'

I said, yes, absolutely kids, thank you very much. I'm really excited to become a mother some day.

He stared into space a moment and mused aloud that he and his figure-skating partner had chosen not to have children, but the idea of a young lady like me and her partner raising a son of his in a cosmopolitan city like London was truly inspiring – the stream of thought then faded out for a moment. He gazed into the distance here, as opposed to making eye contact. Perhaps if he had he would have seen the abject horror that had crept onto my face and corrected himself sooner. He continued to tell me that if I wanted it could be arranged, something could be arranged, he'd cover all the child's expenses and only play an active role in the child's life from afar –

I was so completely blindsided by this that I wasn't sure if he was being serious. I just nodded along, mumbling vague agreements as opposed to flipping the bench we sat on in utter fury while screaming that even if CB was a woman I would not want anything to do with his gene-pool, please and thank you, now get out of my sight. I allowed this to happen until the reading started up, and we did not have to continue to wherever he was leading that absolute train-wreck of a conversation.

He had been so embarrassed to find CB both male-identified and -bodied that he emailed me and offered to take me for a drink and a chat to make up for it. So who was I, really, to make judgements for this honest mistake? I held a lot of respect for his achievements and position in the world of professional figure skating, and genuinely wanted to have a talk with him. I am aware that at this point my naïveté may be dripping out of the cover of this book and onto your lap. I am sorry about the stain.

In this little bar in Oakland I am so horrified that I have no idea how to respond and am paralyzed with awkwardness. So I don't respond. I let him talk. His hand finds my other hand and is suddenly greyer, smaller, and he says, 'Your voice is so beautiful,' and begins to recite a vaguely nationally prejudiced spiel about Celtic mysticism and my red hair, and is basically calling me a sexy leprechaun. I don't know where to look so I look at his hand again, and it is a paw now for sure, a paw with a thumb. The eyes that wouldn't meet mine only a week before on a bench in Golden Gate Park, as he suggested being the surrogate father of a hypothetical child to be borne by me, were now staring into me greedily.

I realize then that I am a shiny trash can full of meat. I am here to be knocked down and broken into. He offers me another glass of wine, nose pink, elongating, suddenly something like a snout, almost cattish, almost badger. I say water will be fine. I must be going soon. Nonsense, he laughs, and I realize he is on his fifth Bullet with one cube of ice. As he walks to the bar he is a raccoon in a white linen shirt and suit pants, his striped tail swishing casually behind him.

I do not leave for another hour because I do not know how to tell him he is terrible and to think of his wife, oh, I mean, professional figure-skating partner. When he asks me to run away with him, I tell him I've just run away. He tells me young men are bad lovers.

I tell him he's been sleeping with the wrong young men. He thinks this is charming and that my hair is beautiful. That I look like his first girlfriend. She died recently. I remind him of her. Something about Andy Warhol too. So mystical, that accent. So mystical. He is a six-foot raccoon and I am a shiny trash can.

I suppose you could be very cruel, he says to me.

You're not wrong, I reply.

III

When the raccoon shows up, I am in tears. I am in the back lounge of a small bar on the intersection between Valencia and Market with approximately seventy other drunken Saturday-night bodies. It is dark and sweaty. I am so moved and overcome and have consumed exactly the correct measure of martini to feel like a goddamn parade.

There is a grand piano in the corner being played by an older gentleman in a suit. At the microphone stand there is a blond shepherdess-looking pastoral-faced babe in a tie-dye T-shirt singing in a voice that I am pretty sure is classically trained, 'Up where they walk, up where they run, up where they stay all day in the sun, wandering free, wish I could be –'

I am sharing the pianist's songbook with a skinny, young couple of boys who decide to sign up to sing 'Suddenly Seymour', the ballad duet from the musical *Little Shop of Horrors*. They ask me what I'll sing. I am too stupefied by the fact that a karaoke piano bar with Disney songs on the roster actually exists in the world to answer correctly. I don't want to get up there – I just want to feel all this.

This was the spot-lit cave I had imagined as a child, while breathily crooning off-key Liza Minnelli songs into a hairbrush at the mirror in my grandmother's spare room. In this moment I finally have the chance to become her. The chance to become Peggy Lee, Dusty Springfield, Ariel the Little Mermaid – and it is too big a feat. I can't sign up. Not now, not this suddenly. How was I to know that tonight would be the night it would all come true? This was the bar I'd been dreaming of since Jessica first stuck her impossibly long and flawless cartoon leg out from behind the red curtains in *Who Framed Roger Rabbit* and entirely transformed my life goals forever. At five I gave up all hopes of being a vet who tended to sick animals and truly felt my calling was to be a fabulous jazz singer in a bar just like this one. So no. I was not ready. Not tonight. It was all too much. I would return prepared, and tonight would just revel in the confetti of finding a place where I truly belonged.

'Your call,' says one of the tall, skinny boys.

He and his boyfriend move through the tapestry of figures to the piano to sign up as the tie-dye milkmaid crescendos into, 'Out of the sea, wish I could be, part of your world –' and the pianist ripples the last few bars and the room explodes into a passionate, raucous applause. The blonde lady waves to the crowd and disappears, and without missing a beat the pianist begins hammering out the unmistakable opening bars to 'Under the Sea' and the entire bar, composed of fully grown over-twenty-one adults, bursts into song along with him.

I sing with them, and am so happy I could power an entire village with my electricity. I am a hundred feet tall and have been waiting for this moment all my life. The heightened collective joy of this whole room of people and martinis and songs from the soundtracks of our childhoods is holy and miraculous. I am dancing alone like a wild kid, all arms and elbows and my face hurts from this smiling and this singing and I wonder will the police come because the loudness of this happiness could probably be heard a State over; let it wake the neighbours, let the cops join us, bring this out into the streets, let's wake the whole city. Just when the fireworks display in my body has peaked and begun to acclimatize to this ecstasy, the pianist pulls an actual trumpet from somewhere behind him and plays the instrumental sequence with one hand on the shining ivory keys and the other on the golden horn. If the room was gunpowder, that move was the spark.

I need to tell someone. CB and Scott are in the corner talking about movies, somehow oblivious to all of this, and I lean in to the couple of boys who have now returned to their spot, and I say, teary eyed with laughter, 'I think I'm dying!'

One replies, 'Oh, honey. You're just being born.'

I laugh so big because this is so true, and as I look to the piano the raccoon is conducting the audience, lying in the large martini glass full of tips, his fist full of green dollars.

IV

I am standing on a World War II aircraft carrier in Alameda Bay when I see the raccoon. In fact I see several raccoons, which multiply until I am surrounded, and I clutch my plastic wine glass until it snaps, spilling thick punch on my bare legs.

The aircraft carrier is, on this particular day, the site of the annual summer party thrown by the tech company CB works for. This company employs a little over two thousand people, a large percentage of whom are between thirty-five and twenty-two years old. The aircraft carrier is quite literally decked out like a funfair, with large bouncy-castles and a Ferris wheel splashing hysterical colour onto the marine grey of its ancient paint. It might be the biggest thing I ever saw, as I toddle past the free hot-dog stand and free ice-cream booth pointing my camera up at the Big Drop in awe. Usually this cavernous watercraft acts as a military museum, but not today – oh no, today it is a playground for Silicon Valley's best and brightest. And their other halves.

There are loud, excited conversations on all sides as we enter the belly of the enormous old steel whale and explore, picking up plates of free pulled pork, mac and cheese, wine, wine, some melon on a stick, some popcorn, some more wine – I wonder why they are feeding us so insistently. I clutch onto CB's hand and ask him is this what work is like. He tells me, 'Kind of, only with work instead of, like, a funfair. Lots of people. Lots of things going on. That's how they get us to, like, change the world or something,' he says.

We stand on a great platform on the side of the boat/building/colossus and it rises to bring us to the top deck where the booze continues to flow and everyone is standing around wearing thick-framed glasses and having conversations about things I don't understand. We wait in line for forty-five minutes to stand on a green patch of false grass at the very edge of the deck and dramatically hit golfballs into the horizon of San Francisco. We don't make it there, because every person who reaches the top of the line is so moved by the process of hitting golfballs into the horizon of San Francisco that they take ten minutes to absorb the moment and immortalize it – by taking photographs, uploading them onto their social network and writing a status update – and weep briefly into the arms of whoever they are with because San Francisco is just, just so beautiful and they can't, they can't believe this is their life.

I am surrounded by decadence but bored out of my mind. CB is too, but there's no way for us to get back to the city until they start running shuttle buses again, which won't be for another hour. We stand with his co-workers, who continue to talk about things I have no idea about, and I haven't got the strength to make conversations with their girlfriends and wives, who chat to one another like old friends, like they really know each other, and I wonder how long it will take me to forge friendships with women like that, so casual, so how's yoga going, so where did you get those shoes, so did you hear about Cindy's twins, so you'll never guess who I ran into from Stanford, so what are you building at Burning Man this year – and just like that there are four, seven, thirteen raccoons standing around me, their voices gone from lazy California to hisses and squeaks. I check my hands: still human; I'm not one of them, I look at CB: still human, not one of them. Shouldn't we be, though? Shouldn't we at least try?

I look past the immediate circle of creatures surrounding me out onto the rest of the sunny deck of the aircraft carrier. Hundreds of tall raccoons, gathering at the bar, gathering at the cotton-candy dispensary, gathering at the ice-cream machines, at the sushi bar, at the taco stand. They eat and they eat and they eat.

V

It is past midnight in a back yard on Precita Avenue up near Bernal Heights some time in July when we see the raccoon. Evan lived with six people that summer, and the yard was full of pieces of engines, the stray anatomy of complicated machines, fast motorbikes all. Sometimes the yard smelled like burning embers from the fire pit, and some days it smelled like fresh wood stripped bare and ready to be built into something else. I can only presume the other people who lived in this big old house were carpenters, mechanics, people who built things. We sit at a new table drinking draught locally crafted beer out of Mason jars, under a lemon tree dripping heavy with fruit the size of my fist.

'Real lemons.' I am awestruck. 'Real ones!'

Evan finds this a mix of slightly confusing and slightly entertaining: I met him on my eighth day in San Francisco, and he reacts this way to most of my surprise at America. Evan is not a carpenter or a mechanic but a ringmaster of a writer and event organizer, a softly spoken maverick with long hair and a slight Georgia drawl. He has straight teeth and a genuine smile; he is a handsome, gentle scarecrow. He will become a dear, close friend to me and CB, but we do not know this yet.

As we sit in the dark by the fire and talk about how on Earth it is a thing that people will gather to listen to other people read literature and tell stories, and how we can facilitate that in new and exciting ways, monstrous cats toddle their way around us.

'Is this cat pregnant?' I ask, thinking of how tiny Moriarty is, how he could easily fit in one of the jars we are drinking from.

'No, she's just huge. Just a monster cat,' Evan replies, stroking the great night-time-coloured cat's head before it walks away.

Something rustles in the trees by the fence and I am expecting another cat, but a creature the size of a child's bicycle casually emerges from the bushes and strolls along in the dark. Its flashing eyes turn to us and it sits very still, surveying us.

'Should we invite him in?' laughs CB. 'Hey, dude, want a beer?'

This is the first time I have ever seen a raccoon, a real live raccoon. I ask Evan what it is.

'That's why the cats are so big,' says Evan. 'Fighting this guy.'

I have never seen anything quite like this creature before. But then again, I have never in midsummer done anything so ordinary as sit under a lemon tree drinking beers at one in the morning. Then suddenly, silently, a white creature appears from the bushes and stands beside the raccoon, turning its gaze to us, too.

'What in the name of Christ is that?'

'It's an opossum. They're probably friends.' Evan is nonchalant.

'I've never seen one before. Or a raccoon.'

'Cool, then we definitely invite them over for a beer.'

They sit and stare at us a few moments more before casually walking the rest of the fence and then disappearing into the night. We sit there talking until late; then, when yawns eventually arrive, CB and I walk the couple of blocks back to our apartment. Just a Tuesday night: next day he went to work; next day I went looking for work.

I have not seen a raccoon since. Strange things kept happening, but so did normal things. Maybe that's what life here is going to be like.

Autumn

Hot October or *Pumpkin*

*L*iving in a place with no apparent seasons eventually does kind of funny things to your brain. There are no mint-green spring times, no hot-pink summers, no yellow-orange-sunset autumns, no robin's-egg-blue winters: in San Francisco it's always just kind of gold. Funny that. Golden Gate Bridge, Gold Rush, gold weather. Some days glaring and yellow, other days the density pales and it's just a shimmer, winking at you but never burning your skin or pulling sweat from your body. Others, mostly in the mornings, the fog falls like the breath of a great, invisible giant only to be wiped away by San Francisco's shirt sleeve, polished then until the city glows again. Always, always gold. Always warm, always barely cardigan weather.

Now in October there are days that are eighty degrees, while my family in Ireland are baltic, freezing below zero centigrade, up to their eyes in almost-Christmas hail. Trees are still full of dense foliage, like nothing ever happened, like it never stopped being July. Occasionally one or two crunchy red escapees from the branches will appear, posed almost perfectly, as though waiting for the right hipster with the right pair of adorable boots to snap an Instagram of them, hashtag fall, hashtag autumn. There is no fall, or autumn, not the way I know it. When did the word 'fall' replace 'autumn' in my vocabulary? Tiny changes, and the world is not growing burnt: it is still summertime looking, still summertime feeling.

My body does not know what time of year it is here. It is always just gold, just hot spring or cool summer. Not October, this cannot be October. Locals will contradict me, as they do, because I am not local and thus do not understand San Francisco the way they do. I have learned to ignore this smug know-it-all attitude. Those raised eyebrows – how could I know a thing, I am an ex-pat, a blow-in, I have barely grazed the skin of this city, how can I expect to know a single thing about how this place works? So, if they say it is freezing cold when it is seventy-three degrees, I will nod my head in silence and count new freckles while sweating patches into my flannel shirt. If they say it is only balmy at eighty-five, I will continue to sit at my open fridge door, chewing ice, wondering if I am perspiring so hard I'm losing weight in salt and water.

Some days it rains or the breeze goes icy and I try to hold on to these moments as hard as I can. San Francisco in a winter dress, and it suits her – but like any lover the things she does just for me and not for herself always ring out false. I can see the gold of her peeking through blue veils and, while I appreciate the effort, it always seems like a relief when the rain blows over and bright normality returns. I like her best in her own skin.

It rained one night. The first sign of change in the weather since the first week of San Francisco had wept on me when I was adventuring many blocks from home. The rain was a hint of autumnal change, a momentary freshness. I was walking through Valencia and Guerrero on the way home. I wore a wide-brimmed black felt hat, and the lashings of temperate water rolled down it in streams. I didn't even speed up when it started; I slowed down to take it all in, to enjoy the soak. Closed my eyes a moment, breathed in the smell of sudden rain and pretended it was Dublin. I opened them again and didn't want to pretend any more. As I moved up the hills, the passing cars' headlights made fireworks of the rivers of fresh water on the road, the new drops dancing on the sidewalk. The noise of it was so welcome.

I let myself into my building and up into our flat and Moriarty was sitting there on the windowsill, fixated. A passing car outside had something epic on the radio, some guitar solo. I sat on the sill with the small cat in my lap and explained quietly to him that this, this was rain. Where I come from, it does this all the time. Keeps the air clean, our souls clean. He had never seen it before in all of his tiny life – this might be the first time he'd heard 'Don't Stop Believin'' too. He was born in April, came to us in June, and it hadn't rained since then. Not even a little. I didn't take off my soaked boots or my wet sweater for a while. I just sat there with him purring away, enjoying the orchestra outside. Enjoying the moment of autumn while it lasted before it faded out into heat once more.

In an effort to track, somehow, the quick leapfrog of months in my first year here, I am always watching the fruits that appear in the markets that irregularly frame the streets I wander every day. In the long summer, there were avocados the size of a grown man's fist, with skins of different shades and textures, so plentiful that they'd sit rotting in heaps beneath awnings in markets on Mission, going ten for a dollar. As June, July, August and September flickered by me, suddenly these fat green-brown fists became orange spheres in all shapes and textures: the pumpkins arrived, signalling that summer was over.

I bought one in a supermarket with CB, with intentions to spend an evening carving something into it. Somehow we would magically have a fireplace, the cat would be less hyper-violent, instead peacefully sleeping by said fireplace; it would be so romantic, and the pressures of our careers that usually plague us would not even cross the boundaries of our minds as we carved this giant earth growth together. Our warped and teenaged sense of shared humour being what it is, we were planning on carving a beautifully scripted expletive into the orange thing's domed side, a candle-glowing 'fuck' softly shining from its belly. It was two dollars, and bigger than my head. Maybe even twice as big.

That was weeks ago. It's still sitting on the two-foot square of kitchen workspace in our flat. It is the stray head of an enormous mandarin-flavoured Chup-a-Chup; it is a fat orange planet. It is the first time I have owned a pumpkin, and I cannot bring myself to knife it to pieces, even for the hilarious photographs we will take, grinning side by side and pointing at the skilled engraving on the gut of the thing, even for the pies I could make from the flesh of it or the roasting of the seeds with garlic and oil. Nope. Can't do it. I look at it in the morning and it says to me, faceless, with what I always imagine as the voice of some American boy child actor, maybe a nineties Justin Timberlake – 'It's OK, girl! It's winter! I wouldn't be here if it wasn't! You've survived six months abroad, girl! Six! It was sunny May when you rocked up in here for the first time – look how far you've come!'

I do not say anything back to it, but I feel it with my hands, always surprised by the texture of its skin.

We never had these orange monstrosities when I was growing up, even at Hallowe'en. The supermarkets would have smatterings of them for a tenner or more each, which no nineties suburban Northside family that I knew could ever justify. I never saw one in the home of anybody I knew. They were things we saw on American television shows, not things we had ourselves. Hallowe'en and autumn in Dublin, when I think of it now, is always going to be the smell of fire in the air for weeks, black plastic bags being Sellotaped and tailored into the most elegant witches' costumes you ever saw, suburban cats being exploded, like unknowing children wandering through minefields, by bangers and fireworks lit by teenagers who just want to know what it feels like to kill something. They did it to Helena's first cat once, when she was very young, fed it a small explosive or put it on one or something, something horrific, something that was the first gnarled weed of sociopathy.

Pumpkins are not a thing of my childhood – they only arise as a tactile experience when I am eighteen and have just left school, and one of our small, fierce squad of teenage girls has a car and a job in a supermarket where they sell pumpkins. It is a freezing Irish autumn, we have just been accepted to our various universities and our last summer of aimlessness is over. We are adults, sort of, somehow, but do not want that adulthood, so do consistently stupid things to try and backtrack, to deny looming responsibility any power over us.

It is night and we are meeting Nat after work, presumably to go driving around housing estates and beaches, park outside twenty-four-hour malls and walk around their silence, half playing hide-and-seek and half testing how loud our voices could echo through the aisles before we unsettled somebody, or ourselves. We, at this point, are Louise, Helena and Steph. These are things we did often, almost constantly, listening to the same three electronica CDs and talking about the same handful of stupid teenage boys. The albums we listened to were infinitely more memorable than the boys we spent our time on. They are a haze of bad hair, acne, greedy hands and terribly spelled text messages now. But 'Harder, Better, Faster, Stronger' – those beats still give me happy first-love feelings and place me in that tiny red car with five wonderful girls. It is the joy from a summer's afternoon, it is Nat's hand full of Cadbury's Creme Eggs from the sweet counter when I am tearful because a hairdresser cut my hair like Oscar Wilde's again and I am sure I will never look feminine and she gives me these chocolates and I scamper away and eat them all at once, as though somehow they'll make my hair grow back quicker. These moments are sacred, glimmers of laughter highlighting otherwise grim school years. Maybe they are more sacred now because they can never be emulated again. We are all far, far gone.

In autumn, this cold Irish night, five thousand miles away and seven years ago, we, a small mob of us who all sat at the same lunch table in our dreadful Catholic all-girls school, creep into the ramshackle ancientness of Northside Shopping Centre and into Superquinn, where Nat is locking up. She has the most beautiful intercom voice – her father is English and she can switch on this sudden, surprising BBC public-service-announcement voice at a moment's notice. We stand around, throwing shapes, talking shite, probably singing, probably being obnoxious. Those supermarkets always smelled like fresh bread and delicatessen pasta salad. I love supermarkets, so colourful and dense. I feel like I spent a lot of time in supermarkets as a teenager in the sprawl of our suburbs, often with these girls. In San Francisco some days I still walk around supermarkets trying to figure out what half of the products are, trying to figure out why it costs less to buy six Pop Tarts than a bag of spinach. The supermarkets smell different here, like sugar or syrup or the inside of a freezer. I am not a teenage girl with a gang of others around me trying to find the cheapest pack of yesterday's jam-filled donuts to eat in somebody's car or out in the field, the green in our housing estate. This is a long way from Superquinn.

I am not really paying attention, but at some point it is decided that we are going to take the softening, just-about-rotting pumpkins from the fresh fruit and vegetable section and put them in the car and drive away. They're getting thrown out in the morning, better than them going to waste, technically it isn't stealing, we reassure each other, yeah, technically, technically.

This is not the first time we have done this. I mean, it's not the first time we have taken large orange things from their rightful spot. Once we drove out to the nicest suburb on our side of the city, with the huge park and the castle, to see if we could sneak into Prince's open-air gig. Helena, Stef and I worked in a local cinema with a guy who loved Prince so much his tiny single bedroom in his parents' house was painted bright purple with the Prince insignia (the male and female symbols combined) stencilled on the door in silver. We liked Prince just fine, not as much as him, but we had nothing better to do and so elected to adventure. We drove around the village of boutiques and wine-sellers and bistros and coffee shops until we hit the park, and it became increasingly apparent that there was no way we were going to be able to sneak in. We were angered by this. There were many orange street cones, small enough on the streets to mark where the musically euphoric and probably out-of-their-mind-pissed crowds should be walking once the gig was over.

We stopped the car in the middle of the street and stole five of them.

I have no idea how we got away with this, and remember only breathlessness, rolling down the windows on the coast road home – that'll teach them, that'll teach them, these are our cones now. I think sometimes how annoyed I'd be now if I saw a clutch of teenage girls stealing traffic cones. I'd probably shout at them and ask them what their parents would think of them, what benefit there was to stealing traffic cones, that they weren't impressing anyone.

Though I distinctly remember being pretty impressed with myself at the time; being pretty impressed with us.

They are still in the attic of Nat's family home. They are artefacts now: I wonder will they ever be bagged and charted evidence against us, the least likely pack of teenage delinquents ever to grace the suburbs of the capital of Ireland. The worst girl gang, blind Celtic Tiger cubs with no fights to pick but just enough spare time to be hungry for chaos.

Whatever wild contagion that morphed us from nice, smiling teenage girls into Ocean's Eleven was wild in us again in the fruit and vegetable aisle of Superquinn, and next thing I know we are capering through a night-time shopping centre, arms laden with a pumpkin each – they were heavier than I knew, but we make it, somehow, to the car park and stick them in the boot and collapse into the car altogether and we are laughing and this is terrible and we are thieves, kind of, and I am sure somebody (probably me because usually I am a wet blanket) says so, and I am sure there is a flicker of guilt before we start to wonder, as we pull out of the car park, what the fuck we are going to do with the pumpkins now. They are contraband: perishable – borderline perished considering they were due to be dumped the following day, obviously stolen (why would five teenage girls spend ten euros or more of their hard-earned cash on pumpkins? It is at the tail end of the Tiger, and we have only known a world where we could go out and earn our money. This was independence, sure, but realistically our parents kept close eyes on us, knowing full well we'd still rather spend it on shoes than pumpkins and they would be, no doubt, a combination of baffled and furious if they found out how we'd acquired them).

I have no idea what we do with them from there or how that night ends. I do not know what happened to the pumpkins, so instead I will tell you that we drove to the beach (as we so often did) and threw them into the sea, for the fish and mermaids and whales to carve silly faces into, make pies with the flesh and roast the seeds with garlic and oil. One pumpkin, however, does not get roasted by mermaids. It just rolls along the seashore for seven years.

In those seven years, Nat moves to England and becomes a make-up artist. Helena packs her bags slowly for Bristol to make animated films. I'm gone, obviously. Stef and Louise stay, for the time being, carving their own lives out. We outgrow our old habits, outgrow most of the boys. Three of us engaged. One of us owns a house. A bird. A dog. A cat. We don't see each other so much, even in the last days that we all live in Dublin. I think I've missed them for longer than I've been gone, but there's that thing about growing up again, that thing about change, that thing about what seven years will do. Time passing is a terror.

But, yeah. Let's say the orange thing rolls until it finds a pumpkin patch on the west coast of America. It is picked and stickered and sold to a buyer for Safeway on Mission Street, San Francisco. They sell pumpkins for a dollar but, still, I wonder if their strawberries have golden hearts or some other witchcraft for how expensive they are. Anything that grows from the soil here costs so much, anything that came from the earth of America, but if they make it in a machine it's nothing. This pumpkin was the exception.

So let's say this Irish couple examine the pumpkin, choose it, bring it to their apartment. They do not carve it because it is a bright marker that time has passed, that they have lived in a new place until a strange hot autumn showed up, the first autumn of their new lives, and the girl looks at it every morning before she leaves the house, rubs her hand over its leathery skin and knows it from somewhere, though she can't place how.

A Handful of Stories about the Sea and Also I Nearly Drowned Once

The chains on my arms are how I know it is happening again. I can only ever see swirling wet darkness and the pressure on my chest is darker still. There is always something curved and hard pushing the length of my spine. I struggle against the binding still, though I have dreamed this a hundred times before. I can hear the impossible chorus of the chains and the disturbed rushing muteness of water from below. It is not so cold that I cannot move: the sea permits me my struggle – it lets me try to live. Sometimes I can feel a pulling, like someone is trying to drag me. Mostly, though, there is just the pressure, and I bend to it but I do not break. I do not open my mouth. I do not breathe the heavy, cold salt ocean into my lungs. Sometimes I wake up so drenched from sweat that I swear I have been there and returned.

I have been having this dream since I was fifteen. I remember the first time I had it, and the last time was a little over a week ago. The scene of it often interrupts other dreams, invites itself into episodes of me dancing with F. Scott Fitzgerald and, just as he whispers that Zelda won't mind if we spend the night, the tenderness of his arms turns to heavy links and he is above me, miles above me, holding his martini glass, mouth black and endless and huge – I am underwater and it is very dark. Some other night, when I am a child rolling down a grassy slope in Malahide Park in the honeyed warmth of summer, just as I hit my stride, my quickest pace, just after the hill becomes steep enough to throw me out of control and into the wildest spin of laughter – I am underwater and it is very dark. Recurring dreams are strange things. This is not the only one I have ever had repeat itself, but it is by far the most persistent.

I never see how I get there, where 'there' actually is, who put me there or if I survive. I am, however, entirely certain that if the pressure on my chest is water, then the weight on my back is the hull of a ship. It bears down on me and it is relentless: perhaps it is still moving forward on its voyage – perhaps there was an accident. Maybe I had been made to walk the plank or been keelhauled for stowing away. I only know that I am drowning.

I've never been much of a swimmer, really. I can paddle a little and float quite proficiently on my back: these were skills acquired as a child on package holidays in Majorca, where my father would take me out with a pair of flippers and a snorkel to face the bright, clear ocean. We would lie on our faces in the shallows, flipping quietly along while shoals of little silvery fish would move around us, our pale tourist bodies just temporary in their peaceful habitat. I'd skim my fingers off the clean, sandy floor and my goggles would slowly fill with water. Often I felt like the suction of the airlock of my goggles would pull my eyeballs out of their sockets and I would be blinded there in the ocean, but it never happened. The pull would soften, the salt water would trickle in, I'd lift my head and reset them, feeling that pull once more.

Once, as I paddled about, face down, a 5,000 peseta note rose from the sand like a weed and up into the water in front of me. Think the cover of Nirvana's *Nevermind*, but a gawky, curly haired pre-teen in a Dunnes Stores luminous-orange swimming suit instead of an adorable infant. I thought I was imagining it, but reached my child-hand out for it, greedy for this sudden gift. I thought of the swimming tourist who had lost it and felt guilty, but my father thought I was a treasure hunter when I rose suddenly, this cash in my fist. High fives with my da in the shallows, millionaires, struck gold, let's get ice-cream.

Later, as a teenage summer-camp volunteer, on Wednesdays we'd go to the pool in Donaghmede with our troupe of children. I wasn't much more than a child myself, but all my older friends and their cute friends who were boys were volunteering, so I presumed I'd be missing out if I didn't take part. We'd go to the zoo and the cinema and do arts and crafts, but every Wednesday was swimming day. The vast majority of these pool adventures required very little other than making sure the participants didn't drown themselves or each other. They usually went very smoothly, and I'd stand up to my waist in the cold of the shallow end, splashing and making sure nobody's armbands fell off.

After the children we were supposed to be supervising had departed for the locker room, however, was when things would get serious. There was always a moment or two of a lag, somehow, that kept me in the pool waiting for the nippers at hand to safely emerge, which would leave me an open target for Spencer and Des. Spencer was my neighbour, Lauren's boyfriend, and had become a new friend, and would grow to be almost brother-like to me for much of my late teens. Des was tall and better looking than the vast majority of two-years-older-than-me suburban teenage boys I was acquainted with: he liked Guns 'n' Roses and wore cowboy boots.

They would approach like boy-sharks, quicker than me in the water and stronger by a long shot, all lean muscle and wispy chest hair. Spencer would grab my ankles and Des my shoulders, and they would drag me kicking and screaming to the deep end of the pool. There, they would hold me under water then swoop me out again – 5' 9" of me and not much of an appetite, I was a tiny rag doll those years, so I was powerless against their cackling menace. They'd laugh, then dip me; I'd flail and splash. They'd laugh, then dip me; I'd flail and splash. Repeat, repeat, until we were shouted down by a lifeguard and resumed something resembling responsibility. As the weeks passed I'd get quick enough to avoid them, but it was the same every summer for lots of summers.

This was around the time the dream started to come, but it was nothing to do with Spencer and Des. They were not the pirates who drowned me, sweet boys with big hearts and filthy mouths. This, this swimming pool ridiculousness, was more chlorine and laughter than sheer terror, but there always was a disorientation left by that throat full of chemical water, that panicked, muted 'stop, stop' that would every time be outsung by the splash. It was harmless, all of it, but it did truly show me that if there is one thing stronger than the hands of teenage boys, it is water.

So swimming was never going to be a big part of my day-to-day life. It wasn't something I had any desire for, it wasn't something I needed to conquer, just another sport I was terrible at. Still, living where I did, so close to the coast, it was very hard not to have a fixation on the sea. The freezing pollution of Dollymount beach was never an invitation, but the most gorgeous hush from afar. It taught me to admire and keep my distance. I didn't need to get my feet wet to know that it was a splendid, beautiful thing.

When I moved to Galway, my first time packing my life into boxes and turning my back on Dublin, I'd sit in my cheap, cavernous north-facing bedroom on windy, rainy nights in a heap of blankets watching BBC documentaries about creatures who live in the depths of the ocean. David Attenborough's scientific wisdom kept me warm when CB, then only a new boyfriend, was on the opposite coast of our island. Attenborough's voice became the voice of everything that lived there in the depths, and I would watch, crushing hard, knowing my fleshy clumsiness was as far from a mermaid as it was possible to get.

There's a reason I'm telling you all these things. Stay with me – I'm getting to it.

Erin, however, was a different story. My big-eyed wild-haired emigrant hero, she'd lived in Ireland five years when I met her. She came alone and lived for the longest time in a cabin in a small commune on Bray Head. Her voice is molasses, and I am almost sure she is a lion in the body of a girl. She is the keeper of great, shocking stories and full of deviant plans and is always completely soft and drawling and North Carolina about it, so even if she tried to lead me off the edge of a cliff I'd most likely go with her. All of this goes to say, she led me off a cliff and I absolutely went with her.

When she said to me, 'Come out to Bray and we'll all go swimming,' I envisioned maybe a few hot whiskeys and a courageous barefoot sprint at the arriving waves on the stony beach near the derelict arcades. I did not anticipate, however, reluctantly winding my way down the side of the cliffs, towel over my shoulder, clutching CB's hand for dear life as Erin strode confidently ahead of us.

'I don't think I can do this,' I told him.

'You're grand,' he replied.

I knew full well that, even if I wasn't actually grand at all, in fifteen minutes' time I would be standing on a crag in yet another Dunnes Stores bathing suit, an equally unflattering shade of turquoise with a giant plastic shell on the front, bracing myself for the leap. I wanted so badly to impress Erin. Make myself as brave as she.

I am usually a cautious-bordering-on-uncool kind of gal. The idea of getting physically hurt in any way makes me want black tea and blankets. I'm excellent on the sidelines, a wholehearted cheerleader and supporter of mischief and climbing and debauchery, but by and large, it's fine – you don't need to save a spot on the tree-branch for me: I'm good down here. The constant and unrelenting awareness of my own mortality has done an excellent job of keeping me away from team sports, hiking, moving at a pace fast enough to break a sweat or increase the velocity of any potential fall a dislodged slide of concrete may or may not incur. I like my soft, healthy body. It is largely crooked enough as it is without any escapades making it any more uneven.

However. Standing on the nook in the cliffside in Bray, something in me disengages. All my usual self-preservation instincts had fallen off my body as I slid down the grassy slope to get here. I will be as brave as Erin, I decide. She takes these plunges frequently; she is never afraid. I will be just as courageous as she, and

I will step off the edge of this island and face the cold mouth of the rest of the world. She makes it look so easy, so normal: one foot after the other then splash, her strong body and the whole world.

CB is a pale thin line on the cliffside. He looks at me then leaps, long arms and endless legs. He is always the softest, quietest person in any given room, but he is fearless and constantly surprising. I am the last to jump in. The foam on the space-blue-black waves is rabid and runs hungrily along the cliffside like a tongue against broken, unforgiving teeth.

My jeans and hoodie are in a heap beside me with the trainers I borrowed from Erin to get to this ridiculous, dangerous crag. My dainty pumps would have long murdered me on the way down. I am far more naked than I usually like to be in public. It is cold. CB and Erin are splashing about and shouting encouragement, and I do not think I even decide to jump; rather the earth moves suddenly away from me. I do not brace myself or hold my nose. I just put one foot off the earth and the other into the unknown.

It feels terrible at first. Not terrible in the 'oh, you just spilled your cup of tea on the floor, that's terrible, let me get you a new one' casual, hyperbolic use of the word. Terrible like my world is ending. Terrible like every part of my body is hurting. Terrible like I've just remembered I can't swim, also I can't remember how to breathe. Terrible like this might be the last stupid thing I ever do. The freezing unfamiliarity instantly turns my body into the heaviest weight I have ever carried, and the same pressure on my chest and throat is a galaxy overwhelming. I feel very serious, because as far as I am concerned I have approximately a minute to live. But I look hilarious and am overreacting, loudly.

Erin and CB cackle the laughter of people who know how to swim while I am an astronaut there, barely adjusting, treading water impossibly slowly then impossibly frantically.

She, at parties from now until kingdom come, will recount my flailing theatrically, 'I feel like a small dying animal, small dying animal,' while gasping for breath. I am pretty sure I said this: there is no cool or dignity in my terror. I would have been pretty happy with these as my last words, but I knew in my gut as I fought there that I was not going to die – this was not the death my dreams had shown me again and again. There was water, heavy freezing water, sure. But there was no boat.

There will be a boat. Stay with me.

There is no timescale for this. I am there for fifteen seconds, an hour, a year. CB and Erin's sentences go on forever – they are slow and deep. I am gasping and panicked until I am not, my body becoming exhausted so quickly, somehow acclimatizing. Before I know it I am laughing too, hysterical, unburdened by land, kind of swimming – yeah, let's say I'm swimming – who knew it was so easy! I take back what I said about not being a mermaid.

Then, like a fat, dark angel, a seal rises not six feet from our trifecta of champions. I scream, so surprised and delighted by this unexpected visitor that all my still-shocked body could breathily exclaim was, as Erin will dramatically re-enact in her honey drawl at late-night storytelling sessions over empty bottles of rum and cigarette ends, 'Motherfucker! That is a seal!'

I wonder is it some kind of cosmic messenger, sent to us from somewhere else to tell us to get the hell out of this choppy cove and back to the organized mechanical chaos of our dry world. CB wonders, aloud, if seals are carnivorous. None of us knows. The seal is suddenly malevolent as it ducks below us again. Maybe it is hungry. Maybe we were stupid to land ourselves on its cloudy doorstep, to poke our greedy fingers through its pearlescent gates. Erin now informs us that there are plenty of seals around here – she sees them often. Our new companion is probably not alone.

The water, as though listening to our conversation, subtly becomes more violent, pulling us and pushing us apart. The sky becomes colder, as it does in the middle of all interesting days in Ireland. It is finally time to shed my new fins and get out. The ocean had Stockholm Syndromed me into loving it, and I sadly paddle my way towards the crag to haul myself back to reality.

Erin and CB re-enter orbit, and burn through the transition seamlessly, with the waves growing ever more riotous behind them. I cling to the rocks and attempt to follow their strategy – hold on to the cliffside when the waves push you closest to the land, use their strength to push yourself back above the surface – but my parachute fails and I am sucked back into the blackness. My heart is stereo over the rush of water and the calls of encouragement from above, only this time much farther away than when they were in here and I was up there, cold and exposed but dry and safe.

In this moment an instinct overtakes my body in a way it has never done before. I am fighting something so much stronger than myself, and if I do not overcome it those shining black creatures would feast on my bloated, drowned body then escort me to the special hell reserved for stupid, overambitious girls. I had been sleepwalking this experience for years, so the terror is not new, not really. There is a sleepy muscle memory in my body: it knows what to do somehow, as it is thrashed against the rocks and I cling and cling again to no avail. I am so tired. Nobody has a mobile phone – they are in our bags back at the cabin. There are no helicopters ready to swoop down, no giant steel horseflies on the horizon. No little dinghies bobbing just around the rocks, ready to hoist me from this impossible escape. There is no rescue team: Erin and CB could dive in but they'd stand no chance if I went under into the dense blue of it. Who knows how deep it is here, where it could lead?

What keeps me trying is that I know that this is not how I die. I feel my dark-matter limbs and know that there is nothing binding me. No chains. There is no weight on my back. There is no boat. This is not how I go. When I go, there will be a boat. I will get out of this water.

Each grip and pull makes me more determined. It takes a long time, but eventually I wrap all my strength around the side of the cliff and hold on and drag myself up with a fat swell. Erin and CB applaud riotously. I am trembling as it moves, and feel the cruelty of the rocks on my tired body, but I am a crescendo of pride. Check me out – I have overcome the gap between the cold and wet unknown and my beautiful, solid land. The stillness of this rock is shocking to me, and when I finally stand tall I am boneless and shaking but so charged I could generate light in an entire city. I spit in the face of Davy Jones.

'Sarah, look at your legs.' CB's voice breaks my internal disco of triumph, cuts short my victory lap. The red of the streams of blood on my legs is the first time I truly see colour. It rolls from the small new cuts on my thighs so casually, like rain-on-a-window casually, like no big deal. The salt from what is left of the water on my body suddenly stings, and I am aware that there are tens of twenties of cuts, teeth marks from the side of Ireland, and the pain is so different from the exhaustion, so fresh and bright. I am fire-legged there on the cliff; the blood rolls onto my feet and down my toes and onto the rocks where the waves hungrily lap, still starving for me, like a great blue wolf foaming at the mouth. I had never been so pale or cold.

Gritting my crooked teeth I dragged my jeans up my legs, clumsy, sticky. We climbed back up the cliff on our hands and knees until we reached Erin's cabin. I lay outside her door on tender grass eating honey and plums, so completely alive.

That was two years ago, in a place very far from where I live now. These are all stories about water, and I am sure that by now you know I am telling them to you because I don't know how to tell you about the boat accident.

We were on the bay. The small white sailboat made this noise as it ground up against some invisible piece of jutting earth below the surface – this terrible noise. I do not mean terrible like cold weather, or terrible like a broken arm. It might be right to say I don't mean terrible like a lost dog or a broken heart. I mean terrible like a thing drawing suddenly to an end in front of you, the last wheezing breaths of a sick afternoon before it drops out of life completely, inviting you to join it, opening huge doors and walking in.

The afternoon on the boat came to us via a series of fortunate events. It was supposed to be perfect, supposed to be wonderful. I had actually been excited, you know. I'd placed morbid fantasy out of my mind for the day and was so ready for this rare, gorgeous thing. A sailboat trip around the bay, a closer peek at Alcatraz. Sounds like something you'd read about in a *Lonely Planet* guide of things to do in San Francisco. A treat.

In my dream there had never been any noise, never been any grinding failure, any unexpected steel against rock – now there always is. Always a terrible symphony.

A hundred things happened then, all at once. CB sat above deck in the 'margarita seat', and he was too far away for me to touch him. Alcatraz, however, was so close I could have reached out my hand and touched the huge, inescapable rock of it, kissed its scarred edges, its labyrinthine body, and I am sure you think this is an exaggeration and, trust me, I love exaggerating, but it was so close, this prison island. Too close. The silver steering wheel spun out of control, and there was jarring silence and ordered commands. I held onto my seat and CB held onto his. He was so far. The boat was making ugly, guttural sounds and the other passengers were mute.

The seat was hard and comfortless so I held on to Matt's hand. Matt was holding his partner's hand, also named Matt. They are tall and handsome both, one regal and Hollywood faced and the other all silver haired and brown eyed, twenty-five years together. Riotous company up until the crash, but stoic now in this scene of potential catastrophe. I could not stop looking at CB, who was slowly dismounting the margarita seat as the sail was being disassembled and hatches and compartments investigated to look for a leak. His Bloody Mary was still all in its glass as he finally reached my side and I clung to him, his safe body.

We were no longer moving, and the sounds had died away. Somebody's voice from what felt like the other side of the planet said very slowly, 'OK. We are letting on water.'

Letting on water means we are sinking.

CB murmured, half to himself and half to me, 'My kingdom for a cigarette.'

I loved him completely in this moment. He says this sometimes late at night when all the stores are closed, pacing his lankiness around our shoebox flat. As we sat on the sinking boat, beside the island prison with bay currents that historically nobody could ever swim and survive, he was utterly unshakable. Completely himself. So composed.

I wore a long black dress with tiny white flowers on it, and my phone was lodged between the left strap and my skin. I shakily grab the phone and stare at it a moment. Still have coverage, still have internet access. My mother, father and sister live inside this phone. Should I call them? Should I tell acquaintances on social networks that I am presently in a boat accident and ask could someone please, please take care of our cat? He was a kitten still, his daffodil eyes on the door always waiting for us to come home, tail question-mark curled in anticipation. Stupid and mute and chaotic, the link that made me and CB a new family in America. What if we couldn't get home to him? He'd be so hungry, so confused. He wouldn't understand.

It was easier to think of Moriarty than it was to think of my parents, my sister. It still is.

Somebody passed me and CB some nicotine gum, there being no cigarettes on the boat. It was pharmaceutical and bleach-tasting, but for a moment I felt calmer, even if it was a placebo. The voices around me were discussing where we would dock: San Francisco? Would we make it to the wharf? Would we be able to get back to Alameda?

I looked out over the bay at the boat races, my guts concrete with fear. There were sailboat races out by Sausalito, joyful watercolour chases, dancing away like toys. I asked quietly if they could help us. Someone said no, sharply. I stayed quiet then as we began to move again. In that quiet, my dream was vivid and hyper-real. I looked around the tiny deck at all the ropes, thinking how easily one could become tangled in them, wondering if they were familiar or if my fear was just colouring them that way. I wondered what the feel of the hull was like. I wondered how much the boat weighed.

Look, I'm not so sure I want to talk about it any more. We had not been letting in water. We were not sinking. False alarm, false alarm, we're all good, let's just get back to dock as soon as possible, OK? Someone starts cracking jokes as we move. Relief sounds like laughter. More booze? More booze. I am a sober and quiet thing. There are chains all over me and some weight in my back, and my eyes are fixed on the water, all the way to the little wooden dock we'd departed from that morning, when the world had been a different place.

When we disembark, my phone is still clenched in my fist. I am trembling and the land is so still, so solid. I find cigarettes in my backpack. The crew are unimpressed that I'd been holding out on them. Somebody calls me a stupid little retard as they take one of my cigarettes. They do not know how hard it reverberates through my body. That word is so ugly and cruel and American that I feel as though I have been slapped. I walk away towards the dockside restrooms and my phone drops from my grip. I need to cry but I can't. It bounces a moment, then disappears into the shallows.

The only item of value I own, eaten by the water. It had been shiny and white. Expensive. A stark contrast to my second-hand dress, my grandfather's cardigan, that old cream leather handbag that my mother kept trying to throw out when I wasn't home. The phone was valuable and then it was gone.

It sinks slowly to the bottom, then lies there, maybe three feet deep. A light goes on and minnows gather around its brightness. CB stands beside me as I stare into the drench. My mother, my father, my sister, all in that tiny white electric box. It is beyond rescue.

The light switches off and the minnows disappear.

Shiny

On the stoop of a small backyard cottage in Russian Hill I caught a glimpse of a pearl ring perched on the finger of a slim young guy called Zach. Inside the little house a party rumbles away, which had been thrown with the goal of covering the entire living room with pieces of pink paper with illustrations, stories or poetry written on them, and CB and I had gotten ourselves somehow invited. We were the only people there who didn't know absolutely everyone, and I had excused myself to have a moment of calm outside when I met Zach. We smoked American Spirits and made small talk.

It was sort of cold, and the backs of the houses on all sides of the tiny yard wore the skeleton costume of large steel fire escapes. The sky was bright, though, and clear; it seemed closer, with the virtue of being in one of the highest neighbourhoods in the whole city. Zach had horn-rimmed glasses and wore long earrings and a lean, mod-looking suit.

I tell everyone I meet called Zach that if I had been born a boy it's the name my parents would have given me, and that I always felt shafted by the ordinariness of Sarah. This must have been my ice-breaker, but it wasn't long before I asked him about his ring. I was fixated on it, the bright surprise of it on his hand. He said his girlfriend, Brittany, had proposed to him only a few weeks before. The pearl was cradled by sparkling little diamonds, and I took his hand and stared closely at it. She'd planned a day for them, made a book especially for it with a story inside, a new section to be read at each stop along their adventure. When they hit Glen Canyon Park and reached the end of the book she busted out the ring, and he said yes, yes, yes.

At this point I checked the door behind me to make sure we wouldn't be interrupted. I confessed to Zach that I'd been tormented for months by a heavy, silver secret. The weight of it was smuggled into the country with me from Dublin. Most days it hid under the bed CB and I slept in. Sometimes I'd take it out with me in my handbag, in my pocket, in case the right moment suddenly dawned.

I wanted to ask CB to marry me.

I'd wanted to do it all year – I'd almost done it at his going-away party, almost at the airport when he left in the teary-eyed sleep of dawn in Terminal 2, almost down by the Embarcadero on the fourth of July, almost ... so many almosts. Zach asked what was stopping me, and I let this question reverberate around the night air for a moment or two. There were such ugly gendered expectations of who should be asking whom to marry them, he observed. Wasn't it up to people like us, young people in unstoppable love, to break those?

I just wanted it to be perfect, I told him. Fireworks and all that. Wanted it to be spontaneous and silver-screen co-ordinated all at once. I told him I was only ever going to do this once and wasn't going to let it be anything less than magical.

CB came out to us then and we changed the subject, the weight of the secret heavier still. I had no idea what I was going to do. Nobody I knew had ever done this before – the conversation I'd had with Zach was the first time I'd had that connection. Nobody I was friends with had ever gotten married. In a way, I took comfort in this fact, knowing I wasn't following in anyone's footsteps.

This had all come about because a girl I had known since I was fifteen, Dee, had exiled herself to Rotterdam on a gap year to apprentice herself to a jeweller. Dee and I share a legacy in having known and dated through the same group of boys when we were around fifteen to twenty. She was a blonde vegetarian make-up artist, features which, at the time, secured my perpetual awe of her. When we outgrew those boys we managed to stay in touch with one another, and one day on a casual afternoon scroll through Facebook I noticed that she had uploaded some images from her portfolio. All minimal, beautiful designs for rings and necklaces, amongst which was a ring designed to mimic the linear formations of the Beckett Bridge over the Liffey.

My first thought went to CB, how his tallness, the straight lines of him were so in keeping with this kind of design in gold and silver. He's not the jewellery sort, really, all cotton and denim and flannel boyishness. I almost discarded the idea completely.

Well, he'd wear a wedding ring, wouldn't he? We were … going to get married at some point, weren't we? Was that a thing I could make happen?

I immediately wrote a message to Dee. This is exactly what I said:

'dee, this is a ridiculous question
like it's proper ridiculous but i'm going to throw
it out there
do you do rings for lads?'

It isn't really a ridiculous question to ask a jeweller: rings for men exist, and are probably a thing that people request regularly. But the word was ridiculous because the idea was just that, or seemed just that – did this mean I was going to ask CB to be my husband? Like, really? Would he say no? What if he did say no, would we just, like, break up? Was I happy to take this risk and just do it anyway? Still, the conversation that spawned the ring started as casually as that. Like I hadn't just decided to propose to my boyfriend.

Over weeks in the privacy of that little chat box, Dee and I exchanged ideas for the ring, which developed into sketches and photographs, alongside stories about how our lives have changed. She painted my face once for her make-up portfolio. We sat in silence, and the brush was cold on my face.

This was in February, before CB had even gone on ahead of me to start setting the scaffolding for our new life.

While we were designing it, Dee asked me if there was anything of special significance to our relationship. Any sign, any symbol, anything we could incorporate to put a story into the ring itself. I told her yes.

I hastily scribbled three triangles linked together onto a piece of paper, snapped a quick photo with my phone and told her they're a … thing. A thing from a video game. It means a lot, I told her. She believed me and didn't question it, despite my obvious embarrassment. (I don't make a secret of my interest in and upbringing with video games, but am well seasoned to the fact that people often react negatively to the fact that my interests could be seen to fairly accurately mirror those of a teenage boy.)

CB and I played a lot of video games in the early days of our relationship – sorry, that's a lie. We play a lot of video games in general. After our first date we sat up all night eating pizza and playing *Mario Kart*. To this day we'll regularly spend an evening shouting down pixellated villains on our television: some couples go salsa dancing; CB and I murder dragons. Different strokes for different folks.

I feel that playing video games with people is an excellent way to get to know them – you can tell a lot about a person by how they venture, fight or race through imaginary worlds. What kind of an explorer they are, if they are a good companion, a follower or a leader. If they are curious or fearless or both at different times, the right times or the wrong times. If they are miserly or generous with control, with time, with themselves. This all goes to show character. Eventually, it goes to show compatibility – how has my journey saving this digital world been with this person? Would I do it again? What kind of hero does this person make? One that wants to save themselves? Save me? Or someone I can save the universe with?

All of this goes to say that I knew CB would understand immediately what the three interlinked triangles on the ring meant – that not only was he my hero, but for the first time in my life I felt like I could be one too.

I suppose people think it's pretty old fashioned to get married young. It isn't exactly a thing twenty-five-year-olds really do any more, is it? But CB and I had emigrated together and were about to be faced with a dilemma. The following year my visa would run out and his wouldn't. I had twelve months; he had up to five years. We would either have to cut our American adventure short or choose to go on together in a very serious way. Sign some papers, make some promises. We both knew this was on the horizon, but neither of us had quite yet pointed at it and said, look, there's a thing we have to think about at some point, and yet the silence wasn't discomforting. We'd figure it out, we told each other, all wry smiles. All, 'your move, sir'; 'your move, miss.'

On one of the last middle-aged-lady-style power-walks I take down the Dollymount coast before I leave, Helena comes with me. She and I have been friends since we were fourteen and were inseparable for many years. She is an ex-ballet dancer with beautiful teeth and hands that could always draw life into anything. She was the first person I ever knew who understood what I meant when I said I wanted to tell stories. She's an animator now, but still a hopeless romantic, eyes full of tears of shock and awe when I tell her I'm going to ask CB to marry me. We talk about how we never expected to be adults so fast, how the landscape we walk through is exactly the same as suburbia always was when we were tormented mad teenage girls, but how different we are, how suddenly women. She is overwhelmed with joy, and I tell her that when we figure out how to have a wedding I'd like her to be my maid of honour and she says yes, yes, yes, and we cry for a while, holding each other on the sandy path by the beach as the sun burns into St Anne's Park, colouring the sky above the trees all pastel pink and lavender, the colour of teenage-girl bedrooms.

When she lets me go and takes off her glasses to wipe her eyes she asks if I'm sure. Not if I'm sure about CB, but sure about doing the proposing.

'Are you sure you could, you know, live with never having been proposed to?'

I tell her I'm sure, but I'm not sure that I could live knowing I'd missed the chance to give the dude I love the biggest surprise of his life. When the day finally arrives that I do propose to CB, I miss her the most.

Look, it's not like I picked the day in advance, so I suppose it surprised me too. It's not like if you'd asked me the night before was tomorrow the special day, I'd have wholeheartedly said, yes, absolutely. I have this whole speech written out. And the sky-writer is going to be safely out of the sky by the time the fireworks display starts – also you simply must have brunch with the string quartet guys: they're an absolute scream. In fact, I would have probably asked you what you were talking about. I didn't decide the week before, or the day or night before. I just sort of decided a few hours before it happened that I was really tired of waiting for right moments and right circumstances and was at a point where I didn't even know what that meant any more: all I knew was that if I didn't give him that shiny ring soon I was going to crack up.

I was halfway down Mission Street on my way to Anna's Linen to get some more bed sheets, due to the fact that the cat had casually thrown up on the ones we presently had in use and of course all the rest were in the laundry, when it hit me like a tonne of fresh sheets that I was going to have to ask CB to marry me that day. No reason. It was just there in my head as I wandered past 24ᵗʰ Street. It was going to happen and that was that. I wasn't waiting any longer. I was sick of it. There was never going to be a perfect time or a perfect circumstance because there was no such thing as perfect – and if there was, this lad was as close to it as I had ever known. Perfection seems so sterile and boring in contrast with the sudden raw realization that today was right, everything was right, regardless.

That evening we were due to help out at Quiet Lightning, the literary event that had basically brought us all of our friends. It is a monthly submission-based reading series that skips from location to location around San Francisco and publishes a book for every show. It runs like a mixtape: no introductions, and every show is thematically cohesive. This time, this balmy October night, the show was due to be at the Conservatory of Flowers in Golden Gate Park.

We'd been there before for Quiet Lightning in the summertime, and the reading had been held just outside the building in the evening heat. The Conservatory is a great domed greenhouse made of white painted steel and glass sitting regally in a carefully groomed nook of the vast park. From outside it looks as though it might have been crocheted from a great spool of thread into a building made of lace. It almost takes the shape of a palace, with a great central dome and two long wings spanning out on each side, completing in little bulb-shaped atriums with smaller domes of their own. It is a grand, almost austere thing on the outside, but once you step inside it is a hot miniature jungle, teeming with life.

A single pathway leads through the almost other-worldly lushness and greenery, all thick leaves and shocking flowers. The air is dense and wet. There are ponds and trees and, in one wing, great *Jurassic Park*-looking sculptures of dinosaurs. It had been a lovely venue to work at, given all the venues we'd organized shows in and seen over the couple of years CB and I had known each other. We met through a storytelling series, Milk and Cookie stories, where we both volunteered back in Dublin, and initially became acquainted while skiving off during the show to talk outside. On the way to the Conservatory of Flowers on the eighth of October, I said to Scott, who sweetly gave me a ride there in his big white car, 'Funny how these things work out. That's where we started off, hiding outside while stories were being told inside, and it was where things were going to – well, whatever this was. Continue. He's never going to see it coming,' I cackled to Scott, who was surprised but delighted to be the first other person who knew what was about to happen.

Time passes. My hands sweat. The box weighs a metric tonne. I don't make eye contact with anyone. I have a secret.

I know that we did our job for the night, taking donations and saying hello, passing out postcards with the line-up and monthly artwork, answering questions. I know my stomach was full of birds, but everything felt like it was supposed to be this exact way. I knew CB was suspicious, but didn't say anything. I know he definitely thought for a moment that I was going to break up with him.

I know that when I took him by the hand when the show started, in a very extravagant gazebo outside the conservatory, and told him to come with me, that he did so without questioning. I know that I was aiming, with my terrible, coward legs, to get us to the atrium where the dinosaurs stood eternally posed like the great warriors they are. I know that proposing under the T. Rex would have been great, but halfway there I couldn't not talk any more, I couldn't not act any more. The ring was so heavy in my pocket and I had been carrying it so long. We were beside a small pond when he asked me what was going on, and I couldn't find words to tell him, so instead led him to a little bench next to, of all things, a pineapple bush. A ridiculous pineapple bush and an emergency exit.

There was nothing I had planned to say because words are small and useless when there is an aviary inside you and each bird is him, each feather, each talon, each blinking eye. There was nothing to say because the adventure had already long begun, and I just wanted him to continue it with me for as long as we can. There was nothing to say, so I took out the little blue box and opened it. He stared long and hard at me, then I realized I had forgotten to get down on one knee, so I did.

'Here is a shiny thing for you,' I told him, voice broken with the flight of birds from my throat and into the conservatory around us.

CB looked at me, and the ring in the box, then took hold of me and kissed me. He stopped, as if he'd forgotten something, shouted, 'Yes, of course, yes,' then kissed me again. I cried into his face and we just leaned against each other's foreheads for a while, and the atrium was empty except for us and those hundreds of thousands of birds, their feathers making the air softer, changing it.

At some point as we held each other the intermission of the show began, and crowds of people began to spill from the gazebo into the conservatory. CB and I sat on the floor holding each other and people walked by, not seeing us or what was happening, not seeing the birds, but that was fine. It was so busy and they were all laughing and chattering the way that literati crowds do, poking at the flowers and taking pictures to upload to the internet immediately, hashtag flowers, hashtag beautiful, checking in at the location like a storm of lives rolling past our moment there on the tiles.

Still as always in CB's arms, in Ceri's arms, I am still and peaceful like the whole world is a cyclone and he is at its eye. This is something I always knew, this safe spot in the midst of the wild. This found, within all this lost. This adventurer who grabbed my wrist and took me across the ocean.

We did the leaving home at the break of dawn part of the story. Now we just had to go and chase down the horizon.

Nobody Told Me an Arts Degree Would Make Me Unemployable or The Cover Letter I Never Sent

Dear Google, dear Facebook, dear promising, highly funded start-up with free snacks, daily massages and arcade machines, dear city library, dear public school, dear literary journal, dear culture magazine, dear private-detective agency, dear video-game production company, dear non-profit after non-profit after non-profit,

My name is Sarah Griffin and I saw your advertisement on the writing/editing jobs listings on Craigslist, which I spend approximately four hours a day staring sadly into, writing letters just like this one, hitting refresh, refresh, refresh. Craigslist is a funny thing, isn't it? Full of things for sale and rooms to rent, pets up for adoption, thousands of missed encounters and pleas for one-night stands. Still, there amongst the Wild West of it, I came upon your call for applicants. Your advertisement spoke to me, clear as running water from a shining American faucet.

This, I told myself as I read through it, would be the career that would make my parents proud, this is what I went to college for, this is why I truly came to America! This job, like no other, could finally turn the asphalt and concrete and perpetually difficult hills of San Francisco from grey to bright, shining gold! I am so excited to be applying for this role that as I write I cannot help but be overcome by tears of anticipation: they are rolling down my pasty cheeks this very moment. I may or may not be already drinking a toast to my success in even finding an opportunity as perfect for me as this one, let alone the potential forthcoming interview or, heaven's mercy, imagine, future career! Let me pour you some of this Scotch and we will toast our possible future together, shall we? Clink, clink, that's right, here we go.

I believe, honestly and from the bottom of my gut, that the role of junior copywriter/localization specialist/receptionist/product-writer/intern/intern/intern/intern is perfect for me, based on my education, background and life experience. As you can see from my both entirely truthful and highly decorated resumé, cleverly ornamented with up-to-date corporate buzzwords such as 'strategy' and 'interface' and other terms that the acquaintances I have with real actual work experience suggested I place here and there in order to appear more employable, I am entirely in tune with the ever-changing corporate language of this country. Oh, recruiter from HR, my new pal, I want to breathe the air that you do. I want to feel the sun above the fog and be freckled by the warm promises of American employment. Everything I have ever done in my life has led me to the moment at which I locked eyes with the un-clicked link of yours, there, like a beacon in the endless whiteness of Craigslist.

What do I know about your company and how am I so sure it is a good fit for me? Let me tell you something, brand new recruiter friend whom I am just familiar enough with to be myself around but still respectful enough to not swear in front of, I know this job is a perfect fit for me. I'm not going to say I'm psychic but, let's face it, I basically have clairvoyant tendencies and this, this is the job all those dreams have been pointing towards. I used to think dreaming of drowning meant I would die in a boat accident, but now, now I truly know that the water I am inhaling as I am trapped is just the sweet, sweet potential of your organization.

Let's look, in detail, at exactly why it is the perfect fit. I say in detail because I am an extremely concise and organized person, obviously. Firstly, I know that this role requires me to be somewhere, ideally your glamorous open-plan modern offices, for approximately eight hours a day. Secondly, it pays a salary, or a wage, in dollar form. Thirdly, and maybe most importantly, dear recruiter friend, you provide health insurance.

You seem like a nice guy. I'm telling you this because it frightens me to the core of my body that if I get sick here I will end up either in crippling, un-payable debt or dead. When the bites started appearing on my body every morning, I thought nothing of them until they did not go away, instead rising into domes on my flesh with toxic yellow peaks. They itched like something was alive under there and, for all I knew, there was. Every day fresh little bumps would appear and my appetite declined and declined and I was a cotton-stuffed mannequin of a person by the time five days had passed. So completely sick, so weak. CB (CB is my partner, dear recruiter, he is very nice – you'll meet him at the office Christmas party) remained un-nibbled, so whatever tiny beast was feasting on me as I slept apparently had absolutely no interest in him.

It was becoming worryingly likely that it was going to be bedbugs, which, according to my extensive and detailed internet searches, thrive in the Bay Area because it never freezes here and the moderate climate is perfect for them to breed their filthy little colonies wherever they choose. They're cousins of the flea and they live in old furniture and feed off sleeping human bodies silently, for three to seven minutes at a time.

If now is the time for you to ask me what my greatest weakness is, recruiter-friend, I will tell you that my hypochondria is a black dog with teeth.

When I showed a poet friend of ours, Scott (I associate with poets, dear recruiter, is that not absolutely fascinating to you?) the great rising mountains on my skin, he told me that pretty much everyone in the Bay Area has had them at one point. Owning second-hand furniture is basically putting yourself in the line of fire.

Recruiter, when you do your in-depth social media search of my life, as I am sure you do for every bright, stellar candidate you're falling in love with, take a peek down the months at my stylish and on-trend photographs from my Instagram account. I know you will anyway, but while you're perusing and admiring the various exotically displayed brunches I have consumed and photographed during the last year while questioning the workplace ethics of your stirring attraction to my adorable, spontaneous looking self-portraits and cooing at the totally unstaged hilarious pictures of my cat – take a moment to look for a photograph of a beautiful wooden dressing table with a great, round moon-like mirror affixed. I adored this piece of furniture from afar for months, visiting it regularly in the Salvation Army store down the hill from my apartment, until the bright morning dawned where there was a fifty per cent furniture sale and I could bring it home with me.

I am a sturdy-bodied young lass, don't get me wrong, but no matter how elegant my Bow Pose during my occasional dip into yoga may seem, I am sadly not strong enough to carry two hundred pounds of antique furniture up a hill on my own. I recruited CB and his pal Pierre-Paulo, who rented a screaming red pickup truck to drive the three blocks uphill from the store to our home. Pierre-Paulo could drive stick but not automatic – and realized this just when we had loaded up the truck.

'Worry not!' I proclaimed. 'For I have a smart-phone and am so resourceful and good at thinking on the spot that as we speak I am sourcing a 'How To Drive Automatic' tutorial which I will dictate to you as we drive!'

Sometimes, dear recruiter, I wonder how I am still alive, but nonetheless we made it up the hill, and those two strapping young hipsters carried my glorious new vanity up our little wooden fire escape and into its new home, our home. How ignorant I had been that sunny day to the fact that I had potentially opened the doors of our unsullied new apartment to a colony of savage, terrible vermin. How foolish, how young.

I asked Scott – did I mention he's a poet – who seemed to know a thing or two about encounters with this variety of wildlife, 'How do you get rid of them?'

'Burning usually works.'

He was not joking.

Like ghostbusters in yellow rubber gloves, CB and I stood at the foot of our bed that night, preparing for the oncoming genocide of creeping, crawling invaders. We were preparing ourselves to strip the sheets, flip the mattress and conduct a thorough and complete search until we found the source of what was biting me. I was nauseous, but am uncertain whether that was from the toxic bites all over me or the fear of discovering their hive and incurring the oncoming wrath of their queen. If we found them we would burn all our new old things to ashes. Or call an exterminator.

We had been warned to look for red stains that looked suspiciously like human blood. Those red stains would be from where the little bugs would have accidentally been squished on their grocery runs up and down my form. They would look suspiciously like human blood because they, in fact, would be human blood. My human blood, no less.

With a primal murder roar we whipped back our sheets, eyes wide and ready for a crawling metropolis, as ready as we'd ever be, looking for danger: there could be a million of them but there were two of us, Spartans, fearlessly ready to protect our bedland –

Nothing. Just some grey lint bobbles on the cloudy fluff of mattress. With the strength of three hundred men we flipped it from one side to another – nothing. Not even any lint on that side.

We scoured all sleeping-fabric for the red splotches and found nothing. This, while being a colossal relief, sadly did not answer the question of what in the name of holy Jesus Christ (pardon my language, but we're friends now, recruiter, so I'm assuming I can at the very least take the Lord's name in vain for emphasis in a dramatic situation) was eating me alive every single night.

The next day I was so weak and sick I knew it was time to finally give in and see a doctor. Sacrifice the hefty chunk of our savings and possible pound of flesh it was going to cost to get an idea of whatever creature was at the root of this issue and maybe also some drugs to stop me feeling dizzy and anxious and heavy and nauseous all the time.

I managed to find a clinic (using my clever internet-searching abilities) that took walk-in patients and didn't require golden, coveted health insurance. I filled in approximately eight hundred sheets of questionnaires and eventually met a doctor. By this stage I was more poison than person. He took a little smear of one of the nuclear-waste-looking peaks of my swollen hives, said, 'Bedbugs?' and didn't believe me when I said no.

'Nothing to be ashamed of!' he reassured. 'Everyone in San Francisco has had them.'

'No, really. Couldn't find a single one. Will the test tell us what has been biting me?'

'Oh no, it'll just tell us if you're having an allergic reaction. If you want me to run the sample from the bite, that test will cost $200 on top of the $200 for the allergy test and the $75 for the urine test.'

'But, I know I'm having an allergic reaction …'

'Yes, yes, that much is clear. We'll put you on something for the blood poisoning and you'll be right as rain in … ten days?'

'But what's biting me?'

'Oh, if it's not bed bugs … fleas? Maybe? Who knows without the test.'

I stared hard at the floor as the nurse with perfect eyebrows searched unsuccessfully for a vein in my arm. She had not asked if I had eaten anything that day (I hadn't) or if I had drank anything that day (I hadn't).

When said nurse finally found a responsive vein my blood pressure dropped like a brick, almost immediately. I was dizzy and couldn't speak and looked around helplessly, noticing only then that the doctor had left the room and left the door wide open.

Now I'm not sure if at any point in your life you've ever been in a drop-in clinic for people without health insurance, dearest recruiter of mine, but if you're looking for the experience to add onto any personal list of adventures you may want to compile, look for the one in the back of the pharmacy on Mission Street. It's a nice, busy Mexican pharmacy, and should your blood pressure disappear entirely while a gorgeous nurse draws blood from you next to a door that opens out onto the health supplements aisle, the whole community will get a good hard stare at you as you lose consciousness and glamorously slump forward in your chair. Do you speak Spanish? Sadly, I am not bilingual, but when I came to I was extremely glad of this due to the fact that every mother in the district was staring into the surgery straight at me. The nurse did not appear to find this in any way problematic.

I excused myself to empty my stomach in the nearby bathroom. I locked the door behind me and knelt on the floor, sweaty and dizzy. If this was my country, I thought to myself, the doctor who has been taking care of me for twenty years would have sympathetically and efficiently identified the bites and given me a sticker saying 'I HAVE BEEN VERY BRAVE' for my trouble. Not poked me with a needle until I fainted.

Around seven hundred thousand dollars (or, like, five hundred, something outrageous like that) and a bottle of horse-tranquilizer-strength antibiotics later, I sat on my bed staring at our cat as he feverishly scratched his chin with his paw.

Fleas.

Recruiter, the cat had fleas.

How obvious, and yet we had been too busy suspecting the worst, suspecting we would have to burn down our home and everything in it, to look at what was right in front of us: a mangy little adoptee with one of the most common basic ailments a baby cat could get.

One flea-bath and ten days later order returned, but let me tell you about that five hundred dollars, recruiter. Let me tell you that that kind of money means something when you're temporarily out of gainful employment. Let me tell you that I find it more and more strange every day that to get medical help you need health insurance. But when you're unemployed, not only do you not have any health insurance, you have no money to spend, least of all five hundred dollars to throw at a general practitioner so inept that he didn't think to ask a blood-poisoned young woman if she'd eaten that day before sticking a sharp piece of medicinal steel in her arm in front of the entire Mission and knocking her cold unconscious.

So I'm sure you, as a compassionate, educated young buck in human resources, can understand my plight here. My vision is terrible and my teeth look like a post-barfight piano and I think I'm allergic to wheat. I really need to sort my body out before it crumbles on me entirely.

Aside from this pressing physical need of mine to get healthy and dentally aesthetically presentable, it is hugely exciting for me that your company provides a place for me to be every day that isn't my bed or the diner on Valencia Street that I'm trying to establish a 'The Usual' in. It would provide me with a true sense of cultural understanding of America, which I cannot quite attain at the moment due to the fact that it is almost November and I have basically been a shut-in since May.

Don't be alarmed now, recruiter of my dreams, my anti-social recent past was not by choice! I'm not a danger to your organization at all! You see the reason I have spent most of my days sitting inside my apartment with my cat is because not only am I presently unemployed, but also I am an immigrant. An Irish one, no less, which means I'll look great for your cultural diversity portfolio and will bring unique and cultured dialogue to the table. The reason I didn't tell you this in paragraph one is that usually the second people, especially employers, find out that I am an immigrant, I can only presume they set my resumé on fire and throw it out the nearest window.

Let me tell you why you should hire me even though I am an immigrant on a twelve-month internship visa. This means you don't have to pay me. You can, if you choose, pay me, but you aren't legally contracted to do so. You can squeeze forty hours of labour out of me a week if you fancy! And I'll have to do it – in fact, I'll be throwing confetti and singing show-tunes at the very suggestion of forty hours a week of work because I so desperately need something to do during the day. This also means I'm likely to work harder in order to keep said internship because I am absolutely aware there are six hundred other mid-twenties post-graduate students with fancier universities on their resumé foaming at the mouth and clawing each other to death outside the office doors for a chance at doing your photocopying and not getting paid for it. It simply means more to me than it would do them, recruiter, can't you see that? Of course you can. Look at this connection we're forging.

Here are all the ways, which are in no way false or exaggerated, that your company/product/organization has enriched my day-to-day life/aligns with my personal callings and vocations. Please circle and apply the paragraph that applies to the nature of your unique, fast-paced, steadily growing organization; ignore the others.

1) I use your app/social network/blogging and communications platform every single day to keep in touch with my mother. She is five thousand whole miles away and your product bridges the swirling vortex of distance with pixels and beeps and little boxes with my mother's avatar. Her selected image is in black

and white – a young woman smokes a cigarette and points a loaded gun at someone out of the frame. How the apple doesn't fall far from the tree. My mother is still learning the nuances of the social network, but her syntax still sounds like her. So utterly her hilarious and gentle voice. I no longer envision her as a soft, petite woman in the landing of my old home, but instead as this black-and-white femme fatale who says things like 'Love u heading out for a walk now hav a nice day xxxxx' or 'Are u just waking up? That's terrible get up and go for a walk' or 'We're all thinking of u here, lots of love'. How can I ever repay you and your company for letting me see her every single day, despite our distance? Let me do your photocopying, edit your help centre, answer customer queries, do coffee runs, anything, anything to let her know that five years in college wasn't a waste, that sending me off at dawn into the hugeness of America was worth something.

2) Your non-profit's goal aligns exactly with the job I had before I left home. I was a teaching artist and facilitated creative writing workshops for teenage students at risk of dropping out of school. I love teaching. In fact, it has been noted in the past that I might be a bit of a child-whisperer. Though my long, boring and complicated list of visa restrictions forbids me from teaching in any capacity this year, I can still

do your photocopying. Make your coffee. Listen attentively to how your educational strategies work – anything. Look, just let me learn; I am so bored and I miss my old students so much: they were wonderful and head-wrecking and bright and it was their potential that got me out of bed every day. Maybe if I stick around with your organization long enough my visa status will change (not that I'm looking for sponsorship, oh no, I know that's the kiss of death in any cover letter, don't you worry); perhaps I can get back in the classroom and maybe forge similar connections and hear stories like the ones I miss so much. At least let me kid myself into thinking I'm changing the world.

3) I read your online literary magazine for company on days when the silence in this apartment reverberates hard off the walls and right back into me and I wonder will I ever make real friends in America who don't treat me as an international token or who aren't obviously uncomfortable with how hard I am finding it to acclimatize. I pretend your writers, with their clever opinions and witty quips, are talking directly to me. When I picture them they usually have cool outfits and kind eyes. I'm pretty sure this escapism is starting to impair my ability to communicate with real people who aren't my fiancé or cat. I'm pretty sure it's making me suspicious of strangers who may be trying to befriend me and increasingly

nervous in crowds. I never used to be this way. I also feel you will appreciate my honesty when I say I am largely applying for this position in order to impress absolutely everybody I know back home, because I can't have left and achieved nothing. Even if you don't pay or give medical benefits or gym membership or free snacks, merely the name of your organization on my resumé and social media profiles will convince everyone I left behind that I am inching ever closer to the shining tower of literary immortality. Let me in the door of your ivory tower and I will photocopy myself a stairway all the way to the top.

All of this goes to say, sweet recruiter, that this position in your unique, special, world-changing company, looks as if it is tailored exactly to my every feature and need, almost by virtue of the fact that it is, simply, a job. Working means a lot to me. I got my first job at sixteen in a local bar and loved every moment of it. I loved my seven euros an hour, my fistful of tips, the first taste of independence, my faux-world-weary, 'Nah, I'm working tonight,' when invited to drink cans and shoot the cold suburban breeze in the local park with my teenage community. This was during a time in recent Irish history known to us as the Celtic Tiger. So-called because we are masters of our colonized tongue and we would never settle for marking our history with something as business-section-of-the-newspaper as Economic Boom. I was employed consistently until the crash and still afterwards managed to maintain sporadic odd jobs to pass time, to give myself a sense of self-worth. I don't come from a country of 'You Can Be Whatever You Want to Be!' like America, recruiter, but I somehow figured that out for myself and learned very early on that having a job meant having pride, having something to do in the day. I'm trying to tell you I have a good work ethic. I'm a team player. I can size a screaming infant's foot, spin cotton candy, pull a perfect pint, tell you what the best video game for your teenage son is, fold miles and miles of fashionable, expensive clothes, sweep floors, sculpt ice-cream cones, spot a typo in someone else's work a mile away on a country lane at midnight.

I will learn the intricacies of your seemingly impenetrable photocopier like a hormone-fuelled teenager learning the subtle nuances of her first lover's body. The machine will bend to my will and produce stapled, organized, double-sided duplicates of whatever you throw at me. I make a mean coffee and have a memory for specific people's drink orders from my clumsy adolescent training in that bar full of gruff former electricians and soccer coaches and their tender peroxide wives.

I understand that my resumé largely means nothing due to my foreignness, and am willing to relearn things I already know while feigning the brightest enthusiasm you ever saw. Please just give me a reason to get up in the morning. Please just give me people to interact with, maybe even become friends with, but I'll settle, I'll settle because there have been too many silent days. I don't know when writing letters like this one and casting them into the white abyss of Craigslist began to feel like an achievement.

Tonight I will say to CB as we sit on our bed, half-pyjamaed, that I think this job is really the one, I have such a good feeling. Could you imagine, I'll ask him, if I got a job? I could really see myself working there, dwindling savings and burgeoning depression be damned; this company, I will say, legitimately hopeful, is the one for me. I want so badly for him to be proud of me. I want to be proud of myself.

You asked me to sum up myself in 140 characters or less. Here you go, recruiter, light of my life, star on the horizon, let me do it in half that – have seventy-five:

I have a heart like a train. A lion. An avalanche.
I will build your roads.

I look forward to hearing from you, and thank you in advance for your consideration,

Sincerely,

Sarah Griffin

P.S.

I actually did get an internship, eventually. Unpaid but hugely fulfilling. The cover letter included some paragraphs from the above, but definitely didn't mention anything about blood poisoning, photocopiers or avalanches.

Winter

Festive Word Association

C hristmas had been twinkling its cable of fairy-lights on the horizon of my autumn and I was a homesick moth, looking for the warm, dark spot behind that brightness. I had had my fill of empty days and job rejections, so when CB and I boarded our flight to JFK I was so excited that the fourteen-hour journey was nothing to me. I knew I'd end up awake for the whole thing, wide-eyed and full of seasonal rapture. Such love awaited. Nothing could dampen my spirit. Even as we waited in a long line of departing airplanes for three and a half hours in the stormy rain of New York's airport runway, I was glowing. Delay? What of a delay when I can already hear the fabric on my father's jacket as I cling to him at arrivals, when I can already see how long my sister's hair has become with this year, when I am already telling my ma she looks beautiful.

I am unburdened by the violent air conditioning. I don't even care about the turbulence. I don't even care that the woman next to me and CB is probably really upset by the fact that I'm making frightened squeaking sounds as we thrash mid air. I don't even care, shake this plane like a champagne bottle until we pop celebration, celebration, I'm almost home! I refuse to be brought down by the seventeen-hour journey, oh no, my spirit is *Miracle on 34th Street* warm, my spirit is *Home Alone* warm, and when we land and I step outside onto the wet steel steps the air is so fresh, the air is so

Cold, maybe the coldest I'd been all year, and the December sky above Grafton Street is spitting on me with hail and sleet and my hands are numb and blue and wet as Kerrie is having the chats with the florist on the small street where the bronze statue of Phil Lynott watches over the crowds of shoppers milling around, right where Bruxelles is. She's buying one hundred roses individually wrapped in paper and clear plastic: they are a hundred kissing mouths all velvet looking, some of them as big as my fist. They're for the audience, you see. The audience who are coming to the book launch of the poetry and photography book Kerrie edited and I sort of edited from my far distant apartment in San Francisco. This was the little book that we weren't sure would make it, the little book we crowd-funded on nothing but a prayer and the faith of our community, the little book we filled with the beautiful work of strangers. The book that was concocted as Kerrie sat on my sofa on Dolores Street with baby Moriarty in her lap the summer gone – 'Do you think we could do it?' she goes, and I go, 'Yeah, sure lash up a post about it and see what happens, the internet is a miraculous thing really,' and she goes, 'Yeah, you never know' – and look where we ended up seven months later: who knew, like, who knew.

We figured we'd thank the audience, the people who were buying this little volume, by giving them each a single rose. Their faith and support made it possible and we loved them and what better way to show a stranger you love them than by handing them a rose. One hundred were expected to show and at this point, here on Grafton Street, we have no idea if two people will show up let alone a hundred, but still we buy all the roses anyway. We didn't expect them to come wrapped but they were, perfectly, like little gifts. The lady who has sold them to us is protected from the cold by a great ski jacket, huge gloves. She tells us, 'Yeah, it's been real busy, 'tis the season and all that,' gives us a hefty discount because we're such nice girls. 'Poetry, eh,' she goes, and we're like, 'Yeah, yeah, we know.'

Kerrie I each take a big bunch of them – I wouldn't say bouquet because of the sheer hugeness of what we carry. We've to make it there quick. Ker is small, about half my size really, great posture and a calm voice and the roses overwhelm her, but she walks fast, neatly, with the sound of her black heels clipping off the cobblestones in the wet of Temple Bar. I can barely see past the roses in my arms as we walk over the Millennium

Bridge with its signature will-I-break won't-I-break bounce because the Ha'penny Bridge is always packed this time of year and this time of night. We don't know it yet, but there won't be enough roses for everyone there'll be so many jammed into the gorgeous nook of the Winding Stair; it'll be summertime hot inside from all the bodies and jackets and poems but I don't know this yet, we don't know this yet, we're just trying to get through the city with our gigantic bunches of flowers. The drops of hail catch on the plastic wrap and refract everything I can see, all glistening, all city, all petals, all

Red, the walls were made of red craft-foam and the rooftop of the little cabin was white. It was like a 3D jigsaw, a make your own Christmas cabin out of Marks & Spencer – you know how they do real nice arts and crafts things around this time of year. My mother is really, really good at that, makes dolls' houses sometimes, used to make wedding cakes, her hands are quick and delicate and genius as far as I'm concerned, architecting life out of cardboard and clay and, in this case, foam.

I don't see her make the cabin, but she shows me the packet it came in after she bought it, tells me Paula (my godmother, her sister) got one too and she has to make hers better than Paula's or she'll never hear the end of it, and I am so entertained by this, but I believe in her: my mother armed with a glue gun and glitter is a force only rivalled by my mother and marzipan, toothpicks and bottled food colouring – that is to say she can make a fireworks display of anything given thirty minutes and the correct tools.

When I do finally see it, sitting innocuously amongst other decorations on the windowsill, it is perfect and lovely. I ask Mam has Paula seen it yet and she says no, but Paula had sent her a photograph of her own craft-foam cabin and it was looking pretty good. Mam is worried about how she can outdo her sister's craftiness. I am sympathetic because I am similarly competitive with my own sister in that anything she can do I can do more hilariously.

It occurs to me suddenly that, though this house is adorable and sparkly and perfectly constructed, nobody lives inside it. In fact, if you peek inside the little craft-foam windowpanes, the house is just an empty red room. An empty house at Christmas time is a dire thing indeed, so I suggest to Mam that somebody should live there.

She knows almost immediately who I am talking about. Somebody handsome, somebody whose presence in the craft cabin will undoubtedly blow Paula's mind with envy, somebody over whom, for many years, my mam and her sister have had a long rivalry.

Donny Osmond.

The man himself, the greatest love of my mother's and aunt's lives, all pearlescent teeth and perfect tan and puppy love and any dream will do, oh, Donny. There has been a long-running half-joke in the Kiernan sisterhood revolving solely around this aging 1970s pop hero and outdoing one another with autographs, photographs and merchandise. This rivalry has included phone calls during book signings in New York, forged autographs, doctored photographs and now would include the presence of a three-inch paper doll of the heart-throb international singing sensation in his very own Marks & Spencer craft-foam Christmas cabin.

My sister and I find a photograph of him on the internet, and Katie Photoshops a little Santa hat on his head and we print it out and cut it out and place him in his new forever home. He stands there, mic in hand, mid some inaudible and eternal lyric, waiting for my aunt's inspection, peeking out his window, waiting there amongst the tinsel, the house nestled amid a festive

Garland, I mean the sound of her has always been this presence in our family, especially around this time of year. Most of the time I can barely stand to hear her voice without weeping uncontrollably, especially this song. I am on my sister's bed leaning up against the windowsill that the moon pours heavy white light into some nights, but it's still bright out now, it's early evening. Katie has her tenor ukulele under her arm and I've my fingers around the neck of my old soprano and we're strumming away and singing together. I carry the melody line and Katie away in the harmonies in that way she has of just understanding how strands of music go together, and we sound great, or at least I think so, and I'm holding it together, just about. The thing about *Meet Me in St Louis* is there's all this stuff about sisters, about sisterly love and rivalry and solidarity and childhood and family and illness and growing up and survival – and 'Have Yourself a Merry Little Christmas' just has all these sad words and happy words in it, words that permeate our lives and project our futures and still reassure us that even though things are really sad sometimes, because being adults and almost adults is really hard, and things change so much so quickly and suddenly you don't even live on the same continent any more – even though all of this happens and is terrible and brilliant, there are moments of connection. Moments like this here, singing really loud, where it's always going to be just me and Katie with our same teeth and same brutal vocabulary of insults and our love, our vast love. I know our parents are listening from the bottom of the stairs, and let them listen because we sound cinematic, and whenever one of us fucks up we just cackle and swear in our violent sister tongues and keep going. This music is contained and shimmering, this is our house and our stage and our merry little Christmas and in this moment we are Judy, we are Liza, we are tremendous lungfuls of music, we are

Mariah Carey is booming around me for the eighth time today as I wade through the sweaty intensity of Jervis Street for the first time in nine months, reacquainting myself with the map of it, the familiar gleaming whiteness of it, pulsing with winter coat bodies. I love this place. I remember when it first opened and my nana took me to see it. I remember there was a bomb scare one time – I was with my nana then too. Now I toddle my usual route in and out of Boots and through Topshop, and there is tall, skinny Tadgh, whose moustache grows ever more impressive, Tadgh, who I grew up and was always cooler than me but still talked to me anyway, reorganizing something on a rail and it's all how're you how're things, same as always like nothing has changed, of course it hasn't, maybe see you in The Cedars Christmas Eve ah yeah take care, and onward out of the building through Marks & Spencer – I see me ma's Christmas cabin on a shelf, that's gas. There it is, I wonder if there are any other ones constructed in anyone else's homes that have a Donny Osmond living in them – and I'm out onto Abbey Street. The rainy wilds and all me paper bags are getting wet and gross, and as I walk there, look Jesus it's Ian, how are you ah great jet-lagged to fuck ah yeah you know yourself see you later ah yeah hope so Merry Christmas, have a good one. This happens seven more times between the Ha'penny Bridge and George's Street Arcade, just people I knew from old jobs or old gigs or someone's old boyfriend or girlfriend, just Dublin people, just everyone. And it happens the same way over and over – we catch eyes and there's this, oh, moment and they are so surprised that I'm home: it's nice, that surprise. Like you're the last person they expected to walk by their shop, by them in the street, like you're a welcome ghost, a pleasant spectre, who knows, maybe something even as good as an

Angel silver is the fresh morning out over Grange Park, all the houses white at the outline from the new sun. Jet lag is a heavy weight on my head and I thought it'd be gone by now, but four days in I'm still here, awake and confused at dawn. I am so tired. CB is in his parents' house too, but he isn't jet-lagged because he slept through the flight over like a sensible person, so even if he were here he'd be snoring his usual gentle boy-snore beside me. I don't mind being alone though. Maybe I've never been this tired before, except for yesterday. I know if I can't get back to sleep my whole day will be wrecked – I'll be a zombie crawling around from party to party, from catch-up to catch-up, and I know there isn't time in this fortnight to see everyone and do everything, especially with this tiredness. Maybe tomorrow I'll be able to sleep better. At least now, sitting up in my teenaged bed with fresh sheets in fresh pyjamas with the soft peach headboard and the flat pillows at my back, I can see my suburb as the new day sneaks in while everyone else is crashed out and resting. I love this place at dawn, and that is a big feeling.

I've watched this so many times, but every time is shocking, and that sounds romantic, doesn't it, even though most of the times I had stared at the new day rising I was pissed drunk or shaking sick or so anxious about heartbreak or exams but, let's face it, mostly heartbroken, mostly terrified of something or someone, that all it looked like then was another bloody day beginning. But now it looks like everything I've missed, all the safety and comfort illuminated in soft morning light. All the square semi-detatched houses, the Little Green across the street, the scores of telephone lines, the neon Christmas decorations, the Santa and snowmen and reindeer and on people's roofs and houses all switched off. Even they're sleeping, lucky bastards. I try not to hold it against them as I watch the colours in the sky change, as I keep my eyes out for the last lit

Star, isn't it just like a star, I say to Deirdre, and it's mad late in the day on Jeweller's Alley or whatever that street is really called – I've never heard it called anything but that. All the shops are closing and it's packed with people eyeballing the shining gems and pearls and diamonds all lined up, picking their gifts or just visiting the precious things they are wishing for. I'd held off getting my own engagement ring, but time was ticking and my finger, empty, had been wrecking my head, so I figured where better to try and find one than here at home. We'd traipsed the alley and I'd only found the same faceless stones, the same generic solitaires, nothing that looked like me, nothing that looked like me and CB. Deirdre, mop of black curls and delicate Galway voice, agrees that the one I am presently making eye contact with does look like something special altogether. I am so glad she is with me.

This one is five busy electric opals set in a loud yellow gold band. It is in the window of the last shop on the alley, the antique place. It screams out to me, so different from all its shelf-mates. It looks like it fell down from outer space, a lost piece of a planet, a teardrop from some distant moon.

I tell CB about it and we go to look ourselves, three days before Christmas. There is no other ring, not really. Not one that clashes so perfectly with the modern silver of his ring, not one that looks so well like it was spat here from the heavens just for me. We wait in a line outside the antique shop to be permitted into the basement; an old man in a trench-coat guards the doorway to make sure everyone who wants in means business – it's too small down there for people to be coming in and browsing. But it's right.

CB gets down on one knee in the back of the shop amongst the old silver and crystal and puts the ring on my finger and I laugh at him – sweetheart, I still beat you to it but late is better than never – but my heart is overflowing. The shopkeeper tells us it is two hundred years old, and I go, two hundred years old? Jesus

Christ I forgot how these lads can drink and tell a story and I don't think I've laughed this hard all year.

Maybe I have but here in this basement it certainly doesn't feel like anything has been quite like this. This basement, Dave's place, where the adventure all really began, where we threw CB's American Wake, that night at the very start that was teeming with everyone he ever knew, and some people neither of us knew, is quiet now but still love-scorched. Not many here, just a clutch of us, Tom, Grainne, Deirdre, Diarmuid, CB, me. I'm in an exhausted ball on the bashed-up old sofa just watching everyone talk and laugh, sculling something resembling sangria into them. We've so much to say to each other and sure it's coming up on two in the morning but who cares – we won't get a crack at a party like this for another year, maybe more, who knows when we'll all be in the same room again with the plans we've got? Mexico. London. Who knows?

Moments like this are precious when the boat is sinking and most of us are unemployed and wondering where in the world will take us with our arts degrees, where will give us something, anything to do, whether to jump on the nearest lifeboat or grab our lover and jump for the nearest piece of driftwood that looks like it used to be a door, whether to stay and try and fix the hole after most of us are already gone. So for just an hour or four, and just a drink or six, we can kind of forget how scary adulthood is, how sad it is that friendship takes so long to build and forge and perfect, then you have to move away to try and build a life. How sad it is that friendship isn't enough to keep anyone in one place, not these days. How strange to not know when you'll all be on one land-mass again, who'll be the next one in a lifeboat out into the great unknown. Who will stay to keep the light on for us, who will stay and make the place richer and more vibrant for their presence? It doesn't matter who does what, not really. Only one thing is certain: that some people won't be here next year. More will be gone. So until then I try not to think too hard. When I tune back into the conversation I notice that it's as though none of us had ever gone – everyone is just throwing the sangria down them and arguing about the latest season of

Doctor Who has always been this strange catalyst for my family. My mother at the centre of it with all the imagination and curiosity of a time traveller (she's lately gotten into quantum physics) is wrapped up on the sofa with my father, a sky-blue tin of Cadbury's Roses on her lap, a glass of red wine in her hand. My sister, my nana and I all sit on the longer sofa. Nana's feet are in soft, woolly socks. Katie keeps making me laugh. This is so good. This is the calmest I've been since I left San Francisco. It's just us today. Just us and the Doctor.

Here's the thing about family traditions. I don't think it matters what shape they arise in, how regular or recent they are. When I told my mother I was writing a word association game about Christmas the first thing she said was *Doctor Who*. And she was right. Anything that can spark wonder into a now-grown-up family, anything that can cast silence over a room like that, anything that can hold all of us tightly for an hour and take us somewhere together, mutually and completely, that's important. How different the living room is now to the one Katie and I grew up in – not only the Ikea peacefulness of the furniture but ourselves, all of us.

The Doctor runs around Dickensian London being broody and eccentric and saving all of space and time, as usual, with a beautiful brown-eyed companion and the Griffin–Kiernan clan are with him and with each other. Our Christmas tree stands majestically in the corner of the room, and we bask in its light coupled with the glow of the BBC on the television. The tree holds decorations from every country my family have ever visited, marked with every year. There are hundreds more, collected thoughtfully over years upon years. Lots are handmade, including small embroidered Santa heads with my sister's and my birthdates, identical but made seven years apart. There is a glass Tinkerbell near the top. A New York taxi. A San Francisco streetcar. A house with a pair of black-and-white striped witch-legs poking out tragically from beneath it, wearing ruby slippers. Donny Osmond in a bauble. This year, a blue glass miniature of the Doctor's police phone box joined the ranks. A little Tardis. Part of the grand family narrative that hangs off the branches of the tree.

This hour is a precious stone, an elixir, and I am healed by it. It is over too soon. I look down at my old

busted early smartphone of an Irish communication
device and realize how many people I have to see in
the last few days I am here, how much is to be done,
and like a clap of thunder and a strike of lightning I
am electrocuted suddenly by

Stress, I tell her, this whole emigrating thing has been
nothing but waves and waves of stress. Cathy looks at
me drily like she always does, all common sense. She
tells me I should cop on and start enjoying myself.
She's not wrong. Cath lives in Japan, in a city up
north where she teaches English. She's been there
for almost two years, and somehow our paths crossed
almost perfectly so we'd have enough time for some
booze and tapas in Market Bar. We poke uselessly at
our food and drink sodas. We haven't the strength to
get pissed; so knackered by everything that comes
with coming home. I confess to her that I don't think
I can hack SF, that I'm worried all the time over there
and I'm unemployed and I don't really understand
Americans. That I can't stop analyzing, that I can't
write poetry any more and all my thoughts keep
coming out as weird essays and big lists that don't
have any purpose. That this whole thing is fucking
me up, though that could be the jet lag talking, I
don't even know any more.

'Essays,' she goes, 'are you serious?' 'Yeah,' I go.
'Would you ever get over yourself,' she laughs. 'I'm
trying,' I tell her, and I laugh too.

I think she's so brave, surviving over there alone, only a handful of words of Japanese to her name. Two years feels like forever. She's after bringing me presents, and I'm there like a thick with nothing to give her. She's brought a gift for my parents too, who earlier in the year posted her out a box of Tayto and Cadbury's and tea. I don't want our conversation to end. She makes so much sense, telling me to just stop thinking about being a bloody emigrant and, well, emigrate. Live. Be a person. Do something that isn't writing and worrying, she tells me. Learn how to salsa dance or some shite, she goes. She's got a point.

We walk in the dark past Trinity College, and it's almost New Year's so they're projecting huge multicoloured cogs onto the façade of the building. It's kind of gorgeous, and we snap a photo of both of us, cheek to cheek, cracking huge smiles. I have no idea when I'm going to see her again and I pretend that doesn't make me sad to my core. She wants to be a teacher, and she might end up in London too because everyone knows how hard it is to get accepted into a H.Dip. here nowadays but we'll Skype each other soon, we will, we promise, sure it's every two months on the dot we sit there talking the ear off each other, staring at each other's pixellated faces, and her next train back to Skerries is in an hour so we call me da and he buzzes in in the car and he's thrilled to see her, he loves her and all the girls from college, and we take her home down the roaring open motorway and the three of us sit there talking and talking in the night until we pull up to the village and her old grey house by the sea and I say goodbye to her and me heart is

Full and I push the small bowl of soup away from me. Cornucopia is the taste of Dublin city for me, but I still have no appetite. Damon sits across the table from me with his scepticism and asks if it's doing me any good, rushing around like this, trying to be at so many things and seeing absolutely everyone. I tell him I'll never get to do it, it feels like everyone I've ever met in my whole entire life wants to see me and I don't even know why, it's just because I'm here, I think, and I'm not usually here. I don't have time. Two weeks is a short little spell; I've barely slept with this bloody jet lag, barely gotten a moment with my family. He tells me I should learn to say no. I tell him this is a recurring theme in my life and that no is a big word. I tell him I miss our friendship. I tell him I miss all my friendships. I tell him that I really feel like I've discovered the difference in spending time with people you like and people you love, and it's too late, my flight home is in a few days, back to normal, back to trying to fall in love with a new place, new people.

Love, don't talk to me about love – Damon has just been broken up with. He does not know yet that his girlfriend will return to him, and it will be lovely for two months, then she will break up with him again. She is an expat too. Lives in London. Is an actress. He loves her. I tell him I'm sorry and that love is terrific but can be really sad too, and long distance is a pain, but sometimes you have to let people go. He knows this, all of this, but is just still in the sad bit. Of course it would happen at Christmas time, the worst for break-ups. I think everybody who has ever loved has had a Christmas break-up, and if they haven't, they haven't lived. It's really over-dramatic because all the Christmas songs are directly about your festive sorrow – I don't say this, though, because I don't think it will be helpful. Damon and I have only known each other three years, but it feels much longer than that, and I've known him through several break-ups, but this one, this one is different. I tell him he knows I'm available to talk whenever he wants. He points out that my cardigan and cords are exactly the same shade of green, and that it doesn't look like I did it on purpose, and that maybe I need to be a little less available, to give myself a break. I tell him I can't afford to. I miss everyone so much I want to stuff them all into the tiny photo album of a fortnight's stay in Dublin. I only get to see everyone once, I tell him, so I have to see as many people as possible.

'Yeah, but do you want to,' he goes.

'I don't know.'

'You should spend some time with your family,' he goes.

'I'm trying. I can't believe my cords and cardigan match exactly. I look like a fucking thick.'

'You do. But it's OK.'

It's not OK. I'm freezing and I want my bed and I don't want to be in the city, I just want to hang out with my folks but I've five more places to be today and there's a hole in the sole of my

Boot, boot. One, and two with a little more effort. It's been a while. I stuff my feet into them after rooting them out of Katie's wardrobe, huge brown leather things with sheepskin on the inside and ribbons for laces. These mammoth-sized shin-kickers were my survival through living in the constant rain of Galway for a year. I never once had damp toes for them and wasn't sure if they'd been thrown out after I left but they'd managed to stay. I needed them here. They've miles of history in them and make me feel stronger than I am, the weight of them enough to break somebody's kneecaps if I aimed right. The little flimsy boots and sneakers I'd brought with me weren't enough to face the drench of Dublin in December. The shining grey wet freeze of it was too much for most of them, and I left the little pair of white karate trainers I'd worn on the flight in the hallway of our home.

My mother lined them up beside my sister's big winter boots, her own runners and my dad's slippers. She snapped a photo and sent it to me. Look, she wrote. All of us under one roof, all of us

Together at last. He's been sleeping at his folks' house on the other side of the city and seeing his college friends, so it's the first time we've lain down beside each other the whole holiday and all we can do is cling to each other, there in my teenage bed. This has been so stressful, I tell him. You're mad, he says, I've been having a great time. He's been drinking pints with old friends and watching movies with his family, I've been doing gigs and running around trying to appease everyone who asks me for tea. He's doing it right. I'm trying to fill in all the empty space I've had since May with everyone I've ever known, and everything is going so fast and I'm so tired, but it feels so much better with him beside me. We'll be back in SF so soon, all of this will be over. I'm starting to miss the quiet of our new home, I confide in him. He agrees. Dublin is mental at this time of year: she's not herself, she's something different, on her best behaviour. This isn't reality at all. We're not dipping back into our old lives for a fortnight and enjoying the nostalgia – we're being machine-gunned with love and it is too much, it actually hurts. We'll be picking the tender, sweet bullets out of each other for weeks, finding the names of our friends on them, finding little messages and good wishes. We'll keep them in a jar, I think, or in the fridge. Somewhere they can be safe.

He sleeps then and I am awake – I never did beat the jet lag after all. I look around my empty old room, through the curtains again out at late, cold Grange Park, anticipate the inevitable oversleeping of tomorrow. Know that I will not see everyone. Try and reconcile that they'll be missing from my life for another year. A strange feeling arises. I think I want to go back right now, not have to deal with all of this intensity any more. I think I want to go

Home is a split thing now. It is a bigger word. It is invisible and it is my dad's face, it is the hill on Dolores Street, it is Grange Park, it is CB's arms. Before I leave again for San Francisco I write notes of apology to everyone I didn't see. Two weeks is too short a time. The night before we fly back out, my parents' house is full of people, all my family, some of the girls come by too. Christina brings giant packets of Tayto and Meanies. LJ drives out all the way from Sallynoggin. It is a lot. I sit on a sofa and don't drink my tea.

It is New Year's Eve eve. We'll be in the air for the Irish New Year and unconscious in California for the American New Year. We get two, but won't experience either. The doctor gave me some sleeping tablets but I will be too scared to take them. CB will sleep all the way. I will watch four movies, none of which I will remember.

When we get home the cat will be skinnier than he was when we left, and I will worry about this and hold him close to my chest. He will be annoyed at us and scratch CB's nose when he tries to greet him. The apartment will feel strange. The weather will be unsettling. Normality will resume. 2013 will arrive. We have no idea what it will bring. The two weeks in Dublin will be hard to recall because they are a sleepy blur. I will play word association games to try and remember everything, but certain words won't fit in because they are too big or the scenes don't sit right. Words like decorations and cinnamon and oranges and stockings and presents and selection boxes and wrapping paper and sales and reindeer. Other words just keep happening – even if I wanted to give them a scene or a moment of their own I couldn't because they are everywhere. Words like family. Words like love.

A Conversation with My Father about Emigration or *Twenty Minutes up the Road* or *Love*

I'm sure my dad is way more annoyed than he seems when he comes into town to collect me. I've just missed the last DART back to Kilbarrack and he's driven into the city centre to pick me up after something that ran later than expected. Our route is down by Connolly Station, out over the East Wall by Fairview, down the coast road past Clontarf until we hit St Anne's Park then a further turn here and there and there and here until you hit the clean stretch to our house. This shining route is the same one we always take. Scenic, sort of, in the way the edges of the suburbs can be when they skirt something greater – like the big park, the ocean, the distant archaic-looking industrial estates.

I'm a nightmare of stress. I've been running around for a week, barely sleeping, trying to see everyone, do everything, trying to make up for nine months and the forthcoming years of absence by spreading myself thin and far across the city. He has no idea why I'm doing it (he's not the only one).

'You're not Madonna,' he tells me. 'You don't have to be anywhere.'

He has been dispensing wisdom as long as I've been old enough to have a broken heart. After the first big hurt he sat me down and watched two films in a row with me, promised that I'd learn more about relationships from them than he could tell me. *Annie Hall* and *Hannah and Her Sisters* – two of Woody Allen's finest. I at this point had no idea who Woody Allen was but that evening a lot in my world changed. *Hannah and Her Sisters* ends on Woody's character saying to Dianne Wiest that the heart is a very resilient little muscle – and my father turned to me and said, see, that's everything you need to know. You'll get over it. What he didn't realize was that that evening I also discovered that poems could be beautiful, that old e.e. cummings classic that Michael Caine gives to Barbara Hershey to tell her he loves her – you know, no one, not even the rain has such small hands – all the things that flickered on the screen in front of me that evening informed me of so much, they laid a foundation for so much of who I was going to become.

Every time someone did something shitty to me after that, or I managed to get myself into a less than cheerful situation – boys being gross, girls being terrifying – every time I was an anxious teenaged ghost bringing a bad buzz into our house, he'd always come out with something brilliant, something impossibly rational, some clever metaphor that suddenly aligned all the mess I was wading through. I didn't listen half as much as I could have as a teenager, all the noisy static of adolescent disrespect getting in the way – but now when he speaks I absorb everything. I aspire to that rationality and always will.

I've only seen my parents' wedding photos a few times, stolen glances in my nana's house. They are very eighties, so probably aren't on display due to the fact that they would clash intensely with the surprisingly excellent interior-design scheme of our house, which my mother has been gently constructing for as long as I can remember. The photographs have lots of powder blue and baby pink. Perms everywhere. There is a mullet or two present. Maybe even a perm-mullet combo lurking around for good measure. In these pictures my mother looks like a brunette me, with a perm. My father, if you squint, looks something between young Stephen Fry and young Quentin Tarantino, with a perm. My father does not have a perm but has natural curls. (I did not inherit these, sadly.) He is really tall and skinny and looks utterly overjoyed in every single shot.

Our mannerisms are almost identical, down to the occasional impassioned stammer where we both have so much to say that it comes out jumbled up. Our eyes are the same shade of green.

So we're searing down the coast road and the lights spark over Howth this fluorescent orange, this fire hot amber, and there are white ones too, dancing away. It's freezing outside but there's a thrum of heat coming from the tiny vents in the dashboard of the car. I think all the best times I've ever had with my dad have been going from one place to another in a car. I still can't drive, and I think maybe that's why. I like having him on the right and me on his left and Lyric FM playing something gorgeous. He doesn't smoke any more, gave the Carroll's up cold turkey years ago, but in my head I always imagine him smoking, which is terrible but true.

I don't know when we start talking about it, but I probably bring it up. I always bring it up because it's been in my head all day and all night since I left.

He sighs and tells me I am not doing anything new by emigrating, by leaving home. Nothing new at all. Think of everyone I know. Think of Cathy in Japan, Cait in Holland, Laura in London, Lauren in New Zealand, Spencer in Australia, Catherina in Australia, Daniel in Australia, God, so many people in Australia, that's about as far away as you can go. I think harder and at least twenty more names and faraway locations scroll past my eyes. Thailand. Montreal. Argentina. New York. Los Angeles. Even as nearby as Wolverhampton. Still, though, still people are gone.

He also points out that technically I haven't lived in our house for two and a half years, so getting homesick for it now is kind of delayed.

When I was accepted into my master's programme in Galway and had to move across the country to the other coast to participate, we packed up my life into a white transit van and drove everything to Dominick Street, together. My hair-dye-stained Ikea desk. The little portable telly I got with my Confirmation money when I was twelve. All my balls of wool and crochet needles, boxes of clothes. My Nintendo 64. We stopped at my Aunt Paula's house up the street for a moment and snapped some photos – let's immortalize this, the first kid off out of home. My hair was the same fluoro-orange as the lights on the horizon of Howth, me and my Dad are smiling and I am hanging out of the back of the van. That photograph is on the fridge in our kitchen at home to this day. The road from Dublin to Galway is steady and long and I know every bump and turn in it, or at least my body does, some subtle, long-winded dance. My dad and CB helped carry my heavy things into the first flat I'd live in. We high-fived and hugged. There was nothing to be mourned.

'Why is it so different now?' he asks. 'We talk all the time with the Facebook and Skype, probably more than we did when you were living in the West.'

I try to explain that it's different. Way different. That America is different, that something is happening to who I am, and I can't get a hold on it because it's happening so fast and in such huge ways.

'That's just growing up,' he tells me, 'happens to everyone, can't be stopped.'

I tell him I just miss home so much. My old life.

He replies, calmly, that that's a waste of time. He doesn't miss me.

I question this immediately: 'You don't miss me? Not even a little?'

'That would be selfish,' he replies. 'How could I ask you to stay? There's a whole world out there. Staying in one place forever, that's the real tragedy. Why waste time missing you when I can have good wishes for you? You have to leave home,' he tells me.

I know he doesn't mean everyone has to move out of their home country. I know he means it could even be one street over, one city, one county, one coast.

'Look, I'm not trying to live through you,' he goes, 'that'd be just as bad as wanting you to stay.'

'I know,' I say.

'It's just I want you out in the world. How could I miss you when you have the whole world and a great lad to see it all with?' His eyes do not flicker off the road. Neither do mine.

We are at St Anne's Park now. The council have gone and knocked down the wall that separates the forest part from the path so the dark, wooded thicket of it is all exposed, still terrifying, still haunted.

Still full of moss-eaten stone follies, webbed lakes, empty Dutch Gold cans, foxes and roses, only now it is not concealing its secrets. It invites night drivers into its darkness, as if to say that now, without the old wall, it has nothing to hide. I ran through it in the dark once, from this side to the Raheny side. I don't remember who with, only that I was terrified, both of us were, and we didn't say anything or stop even for a moment in our sprint. There are no lights in the park.

Park, road, sea. That's how it goes now. All the barriers are down now, like it goes earth, man, ocean – all down this coast all lined with amber lights like fire. There's some nameless symphony on the radio. We're very calm.

It doesn't take us more than ten minutes to get to our door from here. The car is warm against the abrasive suburban freeze, and when I open the door it blasts me, hard.

We go into the kitchen, shoes kicked off at the porch to save the carpet. Katie's still up. She puts the kettle on. Eventually, it sings.

Only Bad Guys Smoke in America or Press Reset

I am standing outside the apartment on Ormond Quay. It is raining and I have soggy, tearing shopping bags in my hands. I have been in the city since ten in the morning, it is now nine at night and my body has no idea what time it is. Today has been demented busy and is about to peak with this party. I am so tired and so gross looking and I can hear the craic trill away three floors up from here. I think maybe I should have showered today or worn some make-up or something in order to avoid revealing myself as the mess that this visit home has reduced me to. CB and Tom stand with me, bantering, being boys. I am less patient than they are, my broken, ancient Irish early smartphone having aneurisms in my hand while simultaneously drinking litres of fresh, icy rainwater, which is possibly fucking the hardwiring of the little machine into oblivion. Of course nobody is answering texts because the party is obviously, even from out here, absolutely hopping. The boys talk. I fume. I just want a glass of mulled wine the size of my head and to see some people I miss.

We went to this party last year, too. The hostess, Rioghnach, is a filmmaker, collaborator and dear friend. We met because she wanted to turn a story I wrote about a tattoo artist into a short film and somehow conversations about screenwriting and silent-film structure evolved into a tender sisterhood. She throws these gorgeous affairs every year, cooks for days before them, all sorts of baked fruit things and pies and quiches and pots and pots of deep, spicy mulled wine. Her apartment is an old tenement house with these huge, majestic ceilings and echoing wooden floors. Some of the walls are just bricks. There is a piano. Always fairy lights, always cinnamon. Before I left for America she bought me a bag of macaroons from Brown Thomas and wrote me a card and told me she'd miss me. I missed her. She is part of the tribe of bright, astounding women I align myself with and who I know, someday, someday soon, will be standing on the battlements of a changed, creative, vibrant Ireland, in spite of the grim recession during which we reached adulthood. She also throws a mean shindig.

Finally the door opens, and in my rushed enthusiasm I blindly mistake Rioghnach's bespectacled neighbour for her boyfriend. 'Oh, Peter, is it? Great to meet you again, heard great things about you, great stuff, Happy Christmas. I'm just going to get in out of the rain, OK, OK, OK –' He was obviously confused about who was

Not Lost

entering the building but I didn't care, just pushed past him and dashed up the old, loosely carpeted stairwell and into the apartment.

Rioghnach looked like Betty Draper, all peroxide, her hair cropped, her frock impossibly shaped. She stopped talking immediately to whoever she was talking to and we held on to each other for a little while, my face in her shoulder, her face in my chest.

She says that she didn't think I'd make it. I tell her I wasn't sure either, but I'm so glad I did. When I surface from the crook of her neck her smile is huge, and she says quietly to me to come into her room so she can give me something, before the party steals us into conversations.

Her room is full of other people's coats and handbags: parties like this remind me I am an adult and days of sculling cheap cans and manky wine in someone's suburban kitchen while their ma is on holiday are pretty much a thing of the past. Old Christmas jazz tunes with the black-coffee tones of Frank Sinatra reverberate from the other room: this house has some potent acoustics. Ri turns to me, a tiny bag in her hands. 'Just open it.'

It is a slim cigarette tin, silver, with a fine engraving of a harp and some shamrocks on the front. I am laughing and crying at the same time.

'No, open it!' Rioghnach is also laughing and crying.

On the inside of the tin there is a tiny plaque that reads 'Only bad guys smoke in America'.

This is a line from the first article about emigrating I wrote, that ended up in *The Irish Times*. I have no idea how she remembered it, but this is a huge thing, bigger than me or us, and I am overcome.

Here is the thing about friendship. Here is the thing about people you like and people you love. For the longest time I thought that friends were people you carried, almost accidentally, from situations in which you were forced to be together and kept each other company purely for survival purposes. Childhood, school, old jobs. I thought friends were people who drank cans with you in other people's parents' houses. Who put up with your presence until someone with more interesting things to say came to fill your seat, whom you put up with until the relay race of adolescence tagged you into some new environment, some new team. Pass the baton and on it switches and switches until you're somewhere different, wondering and also understanding why nobody you drank cans with last summer calls any more, even if they only live ten minutes away from you. Here's the secret: you had nothing in common but circumstance, and that's not enough. It breaks under any weight; it cannot withstand disaster, nor should it.

This is how I spent the vast majority of my life understanding relationships with other people. Maybe it's how everyone does when they're a teenager, or just when they're surfacing into the weirdness of early adulthood, the strange mire of being in your twenties. This understanding of friendship, and of love, only changed when I left Ireland. It could be coming of age. It could be shedding skin.

Here, holding this silver case in my hand, bowled over by the tenderness of this girl, I find my face in her shoulder again and I am making those embarrassing noises I make when I am too overwhelmed to form sentences. Here, this line on a plaque on a cigarette tin, this is friendship. Friendship is when you leave, being remembered. When all you can do to remind your home country you're still a person, not a ghost, is write to the newspaper about your feelings and hope for the best. Hope that someone will give you a small soapbox and let you talk, even though you're young and nobody knows who you are. Hope that someone will read the story and go, oh, yeah, I get that. I understand that.

The line on the inside of the cigarette tin appeared in the article that spawned the beginning of this book. Some throwaway, silly comment about Californians giving me dirty looks for smoking cigarettes somehow looks so much bigger when it is engraved inside a gift from someone I have missed, someone who has missed me. Someone whom I listen to and who listens to me and with whom I share a world view, with whom I share ambition.

This is the thing about friendship. About the difference between people you like and people you love. All through the chaos of this trip home there have been moments like this. This tin, this small silver thing, this huge, immense, unknowable silver thing, encapsulates all of it. Friends are people who care about who you are, what you do and what you might someday do in the future. Like, really care. They are also people you drink cans with, sure, but not people who will drop you like an empty one or crush you in a contest. I have been waiting all my life for people like Rioghnach. She is not alone – this holiday has been full to splitting of love like this, of tender thoughts like this, gestures and hugs like this – but somehow as my face is in her shoulder it all comes out of my eyes and nose and my mouth just won't tell her all of this, only thank you, thank you, I love you, I miss you.

It hits me in that moment that in just a few days I will be gone from her again. Gone from her and all the others – people who really know me. People I don't have to impress, people I don't want to impress me. People for whom I am not a decorative foreigner, who do not hear my otherness because I am not other for them: I am like them and they are my other family. My community. A generation of artists whom not only do I respect, but whom I also love like crazy and want to get drunk with and dance on tables with and cry with over sad things from years and years ago.

And in three days it'll be over and I'll be gone back to those poxy hills and all I'll have is this tin, Deirdre's box of gifts, Cathy's socks, Roe's Ryan Gosling book, a few other gems and memories of exhausted legging it around and the sleepy knowledge that it will all be worthwhile, more than worthwhile, precious.

I remove myself from Ri's shoulder and apologize for snotting her gorgeous dress. She lets me put on some of her make-up to make myself look like a human. CB and Tom, standing in the centre of the living room holding mugs of mulled wine and baked things, look absolutely baffled by the state in which myself and the hostess have emerged.

CB departs to go to a gig his college friends are playing. I stay and drink mulled wine. A lot of it. In the kitchen. Because that's where the party's always the most interesting (even at adult house parties where the bed is covered with jackets and scarves instead of somebody's brother and his best friend's girlfriend).

Belinda comes in and I do not expect her, silk shirt and cropped hair. I go, 'Jesus, Belinda,' and we hug for a moment. 'Great to see you,' she goes. She's a writer out of Longford, living in New York. I met her through her curation of a Culture Ireland poetry tour and we stayed in touch after that, and tonight is not the first time we have had a conversation that has taught me a whole lot.

We back and forth about America a little, and I tell her I'm dreading going back. It's true. I'm full of emotion and the cigarette tin is still clenched in my hand. I hope I am not imprinting it or crushing it, but also you would need a crowbar to take it off me at this point. Belinda is also holding a wine glass, and she tells me to beware the homesickness when I go back again. She tells me she thought she'd beaten it by the time going home for Christmas the first time rolled around, but when she got back to New York after her trip home it hit her so much harder. She was in the shower, she tells me, and it just came crashing down, the homesickness. It was bigger than it had been. It goes away eventually though, she tells me, but just to be aware that when I get back it's going to feel different: it could even be worse.

The kitchen thrums around us and it smells like cinnamon and oranges and pots of warm booze on the stove, but this echoes for me, and even after the night wilts into several bunched conversations around the room and I take my leave and kiss Ri goodbye, it still echoes. The struggle will get bigger again. Bigger before it gets smaller. I am not sure if I can carry anything bigger. It hit her in the shower. Where will it hit me? Maybe in something as ordinary as a shower. Maybe the shower is the universal daily moment of solitude (mostly) where we are prone to feelings arriving with the water.

I have utmost respect for the Irish diaspora who have come before me into America, survived the change, assimilated and banded into their new communities, forged lives and careers and adventure for themselves. The folks who wrung the dream and promises out of America – that's something special. They did it before the internet opened its vast, coded doors to let us shoot texts and videos to the people we love using only the press of a key to narrow the five thousand mile gap. The emigration myth of golden streets and happily ever afters was spawned from grains of truth, and that truth was what I was seeking. So when Belinda handed me this small story, this truth, I took it and held it as tightly as my new silver cigarette case. This was real advice, from someone who knew what this was going to be like, someone who had walked this grey part of the road before me, looking for what shone. I kept it in my hand, ready to look at it, to reference it for strength when the dreadful, crawling weight that feels somewhere between regret and grief returned with new limbs, knowing that hundreds of hundreds of thousands of Irish people before me had done this and are doing it every single day. That this feeling isn't all about me, this experience is not just mine – that it is ours. All of ours.

When we arrive back into our flat we have missed the Irish New Year because we were somewhere over the Atlantic while everyone we loved was kissing each other and clinking glasses and making wishes. We hit the West Coast just in time for celebrations that we mutually agree we are too exhausted to participate in. Moriarty makes noises we'd never heard out of him before as he sits at the door waiting to greet us. His eyes are wild and furious. He looks skinny and CB picks him up to give him rubs and he immediately swipes at CB's nose, leaving a slim red cut. He leaps from CB's arm and thuds gracelessly to the ground. I immediately refresh his food and water.

He does not stop making the outraged mewling sounds for three more days. He walks on our faces at night. Aggressively hunts his toys around the floor, growling like a dog. Looks at us differently. Furious. Hurt. Michelle who cat-sits for us is the sweetest heart – maybe he'd fallen in love with her and didn't want us back.

It takes longer than I anticipate to calm him down, to ease this wrath back down to his usual mild sociopathy. The silence of the apartment returns, my internship not starting up for weeks to come. When I stand in the shower in the mornings, Moriarty scratches the door indignantly. I let the hot water hit my neck, day after day after day. I look at my feet, eyeball my tattoos, how they've faded with time. Grow out my leg hair. Get rid of it again. Grow it out again. Get rid of it again. Consider patterns. One leg with, one leg without. Stripes? Polka dots? Think maybe I should change my toenail colour to something pastel. Maybe blue, it'd match the mermaid-hair pink colour of the bath I stand in. Watch the dye run from my hair in Fanta-orange-coloured streams the way it always does around special occasions, special times of the year. Christmas still in me and I'm scrubbing it out and San Francisco is balmy, sunny, secular. Wonder how people sing in the shower, how they are unoffended by the harsh acoustics of small tiled rooms and the backing vocals of poor water pressure. Wonder when the last time I did that was. Wonder when the last time I felt like doing that was. Wonder if I should clean the glass in the doors. Wonder if the cat needs to come into the bathroom to pee or if he is just being a drama queen. Get out of the shower to let the cat in. Get back in the shower. Cat sits in the sink and knocks the toothbrushes out of their cup. Cleans himself.

Days and days and days and I am waiting for it. The cold hands of longing crawling out of the shower and down my neck, into my ears. Around my neck. Over all of my skin and becoming heavier than any body of water – new and familiar at once, that constant feeling that had been following me like a spectre. I am waiting for it. I am ready.

Toenails and leg-hair contemplation dollar-store shea-butter shower-gel shampoo twice condition for five minutes think about the world a little wonder about singing have staring contest with the cat wonder what he thinks I'm doing then yell at the cat for knocking over a thing or all the things grab towel wrap it on head grab other towel and wear it like a sarong or toga if feeling glamorous don't slip Jesus kind of slip and recover and feel elated by the almost disaster feel the reverberations from the other timeline where I fell and broke my tailbone.

Shower after shower after shower passes. No homesickness. Nothing.

Showers become weeks. San Francisco has no idea that it is winter – it seems to believe it is just summertime with a vague draught. This is both unsettling and a welcome relief from the relentless baltic thrash of Dublin. I get used to pretending it isn't winter. I forget about winter and start thinking about what's next. Weeks turn January into salt and our birthdays are upon us, CB and I born three years and one day apart.

The flat has four people in it on the third last night of the month. Baruch. Dave. Tim. Tatyana. Four spoken-word performers, four poets. We hadn't planned it. They just came – it feels correct. There is a rumble in the evening, in the storytelling that begins, in the small Mexican Twinkie-pyramid faux birthday cake. In how natural it feels, how kind of spontaneous the plans had felt. In the dusty bottle of whiskey from the corner store. It is something new.

I am twenty-five and CB is twenty-eight as of this forty-eight hours. Our own new year begins, despite 2013's running start. We are not jet-lagged or flying in a tin can through clouds now. We have long since landed, replanted our roots. The cat isn't even angry any more – he likes us OK again. We invited people to our house to have a few beers, and when we didn't have a cake Baruch made us one from whatever he could find on the way and it's nice and it feels like there is something growing from the earth here that could be shining with bright petals if it is nurtured just right.

When I stand in the shower the next day I feel something rolling away with the water and cheap shea-butter foam. Some dust. The potential of a sick ghost wrapping her hands around me. The year that has just passed. Whatever else. Pieces of home that weighed too much to bring everywhere. Half-finished conversations. Regret. Guilt. Gone with the poorly pressurized tide of the shower and down into the shining spiral of the drain.

I emerge and drape a towel around my waist. Crown myself, regally, a bulldog clip to hold up my wet mop of hair. I place CB's robe on my shoulders and am a queen of this new day, this new spring.

Spring

Scenes and Notes from an Elopement

When it breaks down I can see everything for the first time. CB and I hold hands tightly as we notice how crowded it is, how claustrophobic. How close all the tracks are to one another. How grey everything is, how steep the falls now reveal themselves to be in the emergency clarity of the white lights. This is the world famous Space Mountain, an indoor roller coaster in the dark, located in Disney Land, Anaheim, California.

'Are we going to die on Space Mountain?' I ask.

'I'm sure this kind of thing happens all the time.' He is laughing.

We photograph one another, immortalizing the strangeness. We consider getting out of our little car and walking around. The tourists behind us chatter excitedly in French, waving to the people in the cart that is on the rail not six feet above us. They're all having a great time and we're with them, trapped, all of us suddenly privy to something so grown-up – how the roller coaster works. CB softly pointed this out to me, how we had just seen something so mysterious as the great, dark and starry indoor ride we'd found ourselves on shut down, suddenly and realistically, but with this shock came wisdom. A thrilling wisdom: we are looking at the belly of the beast.

We have been married almost exactly twelve hours as we sit here, bemused in the middle of a shattered illusion, unsure of whether or not to read it as a bad omen. It does not start moving again for some time.

I step into the elevator of the hotel with an armful of Anaheim's local delivery-food menus. It is late. The hotel is sterile. Clean and dull, some big chain, cheap and without roaches or bedbugs. Nondescript. You know the type. I am wearing leggings printed with a vast blue-and-white nebula, a starscape on my thighs (I wear them sometimes to feel better about having big legs: sometimes I will not hide them under thick denim or black cotton; sometimes I want you to look at them in awe like you would at the universe above us). I am so hungry and sun-sleepy that I am considering eating one of the two cheerleaders who dash in behind me as the doors close.

The week of our honeymoon, it is important here to note, coincides exactly with some description of a national cheerleading tournament, so Disneyland CA is largely overrun with competitive sprite-like teenage girls in the throes of something that means the absolute world to them. I refuse to disparage teenage girls because I was one pretty recently and I feel like the world gives them a hard enough time. They are vessels for unbridled emotion, for true reaction, and all they get is told to be quiet, stop screaming for those boyfriends, be skinny, hate your body, hate other girls – God, it is a complicated time for them. This occurs to me in the elevator, and I think about it as I clutch my fast-food menus to my chest as we begin to ascend.

Both girls have light acne, and more metal in their mouths than a cutlery drawer. The braces gleam. One has false eyelashes that are as thick and webbed as the wings of a baby bat. The other wears a tie-dye T-shirt. Both have ponytails on the crowns of their heads, pulling their hair out of their faces severely, their eyebrows waxed to arch in permanent shock. Or perhaps their eyebrows are up because they are actually shocked. They stare hard at me, eyeballs enormous in their sockets.

I am so hungry I wonder could I start a fight with them – perhaps they are judging me for all my pizza and taco menus, gauging my weight, preparing to make a snide remark. That's what teenage girls do, right? It's certainly what I did when I was one. Maybe they want to take my glorious fast-food menus off me for themselves. I slowly remove my Minnie Mouse-ears headband and hide it in one of the huge folds of the immense cream bridal shawl I am swaddled in, preparing for battle.

'IS THAT TRUE?' Tie-Dye bursts, suddenly.

'What?' I snap, defensively clutching my menus even tighter. She isn't getting them – they are mine.

'THAT.' She points at my cardigan.

I am wearing a large button featuring Cinderella and Prince Charming that reads 'Just Married!' – CB and I had been issued it at City Hall in Disneyland to mark the occasion of our trip.

'Eh, yeah.'

'OHMYGOD, YOU'RE A BRIDE!' She is hysterically excited. 'I AM SO HAPPY FOR YOU OHMYGOD THAT IS SO AMAZING –' the elevator doors open and she repeats to her companion, 'OHMYGOD THAT IS SO AMAZING THAT GIRL IS A BRIDE OHMYGOD –' and they are gone and the doors are closed and I'm on my own again with my fast-food menus, shell-shocked by this earnestness. In that moment she somehow encapsulates the tribe of loving girlfriends I missed so badly in the lead-up to eloping, a bursting star of celebration. One awestruck teenage girl is all it takes. Yes, I am a bride. Yes, it is amazing.

The creature lives just under my skin. It has been threatening to surface for years, rocking back and forth, clawing at the delicate prison it has been hibernating in since I was old enough to gape up at *Muppets Take Manhattan* and know that, somewhere out there, there was a tender, honest Kermit just for me. The creature is all potential, and began with innocent dreams of a white wedding until it grew bigger and bigger until it was almost the size of me, almost the same as me.

The monster feeds on glossy-magazine and blog pictures of svelte, skinny brides in dresses that are more art installation than frock. It dreams of Mason jars with candles inside, ceremonies in bright, pastoral barns in a lush countryside somewhere warm and sunny with a troupe of bridesmaids in stylishly mismatched pastel dresses, carrying wildflowers. A line of groomsmen in equally mismatched suits but stylistically linked by matching bow ties. Everyone has oversized glasses. There are rustic-looking handmade chalkboards with inspiring quotes about love and romance. Moriarty the cat also has a bow tie, and is obedient enough to be a ring bearer. There is a small folk band playing Beach Boys tunes. Everyone is so happy.

The reptilian thing that lives inside me makes me panic. From the parts of me so close to the surface, so close to reality, it murmurs the words, 'Most important day of your life' and 'Most beautiful you'll ever look'. These wicked prayers echo cruelly around my body. I worry that someday I will wake up and it will have become me as I slept, morphed me from the self that I know into a hysterical, micro-managing bride monster, a bridezilla. This creature does not want me to elope and does not want this to be easy. It is composed of everything I have been socialized to believe weddings should be about. It is a part of me, and some days I see my skin is scaly, some days my pupils are slits with the greed for pomp and circumstance, but I try to push it down as the big day approaches.

I sit for hours lost in blogs and articles that construct an expensive, stressful grandeur around a thing that I know I will never be able to arrange for CB and me. I look at the smiling faces of all the guests in the photographs of these strangers' weddings and I miss our friends, our families. I spend a lot of time crying down Skype to my mother, and one day I notice that the egg is a swollen weight in my gut that has become such a distraction, a far more awful thing than it began as. The egg did not disintegrate and the monster was not defeated until I woke up the morning of my wedding and could not stop smiling and laughing.

I am telling you that I spent all this time agonizing about dresses, my body, missing friends, faraway families, Mason jars and bow ties because I am trying to tell you that not once in the weeks leading up to the wedding, not once for a second, was I worried about promising the rest of my life to Ceri.

We sit up late the night before we get married, fussing about the apartment being clean and everything being in order for Michelle, our cat-sitter. We have not told the vast majority of our friends what we are doing tomorrow. There is a riot in this secret, a giddiness, but also a huge sadness. We will tell them one by one in the coming months and eventually make a public announcement. At the time of writing, we have not yet done this. We will take our time with telling people because this is not for everyone to know, not immediately. We want to sit in the glow of a fresh secret for as long as we can.

We do not write our vows until it is one in the morning, when we realize that in eight hours' time we are getting married. There is a heavy silence as we scribble on loose notepaper. After, we place our engagement rings into a small felt bag so they can somehow transform into wedding bands overnight; we sit quietly beside each other in our pyjamas. Both of us are kind of crying. We do not show our scraps of paper to each other, but instead fold them into respective pockets and handbags for the morning.

When we eventually, eventually stand in front of each other under the dome in City Hall, San Francisco, we realize we forgot to ask the clerk if we could say our own vows. We'd been so caught up in excitement, in packing our bags for our honeymoon, in looking at each other like stupid teenagers, that it had just not come up as we signed our forms. Mine are folded into the neckline of my dress. CB's are in his pocket. As the ceremony begins, they are not even thought of. It is surprising how beautiful such serious, straightforward promises can be, the ones that are written into city law and history. The basics, the truth. Both of us kind of cry, again.

A few weeks later we will fish the pieces of paper with our vows, unread, out of handbags and pockets. We will stuff them in a tiny fat Mason jar and screw the lid closed, placing it on a bookcase, just in case we ever need to see them, in case we ever need to be reminded why we ran away together. In City Hall, we don't need them. Not at all.

At the hotel reception, another cheerleader, this time one in a yellow bikini, screams down an iPhone to a pizza delivery place. She is a holy terror, muscles and orthodontics and highlights. A soft-looking blond boy with something only slightly more stylish than a bowl-cut on his head is standing beside her; she is taller than he is and he gazes up at her as she roars at her pepperoni, gluten-free crust – 'Light cheese, I said light, Jesus Christ, can you even speak English?!' – with all the exasperation of a woman four times her age. Soft boy silently adores her: she is a yellow-and-tan altar with the fury of a thousand screaming sirens and he is just a boy; he can't even get her to look at him, so he prays at her feet while she continues to ignore him. I love her for this, somehow, this power.

She turns to me as she barks commands, and we have a moment of eye contact. She places her hand on her hip, posing, challenging me in my cardigan and culottes. She knows, because teenage girls always know, that my body has never looked like hers does, and her gaze is *fuck you, old lady, you are gross and I am Malibu Barbie.* I know that look. Those eyes thrown to my hips then my face then to my hips again. I do not return it. The boy's eyes are still latched to her breasts like they are feeding from her. He is feeding from her.

I am there to inquire about fast-food menus due to the fact that our treasure trove of phone numbers to local late-night delivery spots had been cleaned out with the room service. I know that CB is lying upstairs fresh-shower damp on the white sheets sleepily watching MTV, so I am not looking for a fight tonight. I do not take off my Minnie Mouse ears this time. I do not know why I feel so challenged by her – perhaps it is the last dregs of the aggression that going to an all-girls school filled me with as a teenager rising again in my veins. The ears though, in contrast, are covered in sequins and match my lipstick and I breathe slowly and am not in school any more. I am a shiny cartoon bride and her teenage-girl powers do not work on me. I look over her shoulder. She is not used to people dismissing her – I can tell, I have met her in a dozen incarnations before.

We wait there a while, all of this in the air, thick. She thunderstorms away down towards the outdoor eighty-five-degrees heated pool once her machine-gun litany of orders is done, and says to the soft blond boy that tomorrow is, like, the biggest day of her life, the most important day of her life, this pizza better hurry up, she's starving, she's starving.

Kathleen comes with me when I am searching for my dress. She is from Wisconsin and is athletic and blunt, more blunt than anybody I've met before, and I like her and we have a budding friendship. When she swears, it is a dagger. Her teeth are perfect. She has a tiger tattooed on the side of her head under spun-gold-looking blonde hair. She is patient with me when I am exasperated that my broad hips will not sit well in vintage gowns, even though all I want is a vintage gown. It is a hard thing, I am sure, to go with a girl you've been on maybe eight or nine friend-dates with and help her choose a wedding dress. I recruit her because I am not succeeding in finding a dress, and every time I go to a store alone, sales assistants seem to think I am lying and ask questions like, 'Where's your mother?' and 'Is your maid of honour with you?' and when I say no they give me very sad looks.

Kathleen buys me a beautiful necklace in a small vintage store in Oakland, and it is one of the loveliest things I own. She finds it when I am standing in the store and legitimately considering buying a dress that makes me look like a chubby Princess Leia. I don't buy it, even though it was only twenty-eight dollars.

We don't find the dress that day, even though we walk for hours. I am worried about asking her to come with me again because I can imagine it must be very boring and maybe slightly tragic watching someone you don't really know too well getting expensive fabric stuck around their deceptively wide thighs, while constantly reassuring them that the dress is out there, somewhere. At one point in a dressing room in another boutique I put her hands on my ribcage then my hips, loudly saying, 'Look, this is just how my body is proportioned, dresses don't want my body, they draw cartoon characters in this shape but they don't make clothes for real people in this shape' – hoping that the judgemental girl behind the counter hears and stops sighing in exasperation when we hand back another five dresses, then another five dresses. Kathleen then tells me that's because bodies aren't made for clothes, they're made for sex, and this is something I will hold close to my heart for a long time to come when nothing fits right or looks right. Girl wisdom like no other.

When we finally find it, a week or so later, it is in a great discount store called Loehmann's, downtown in San Francisco. The store is largely grey and has the air of a place where one might buy tablecloths or tea-cosies. That is to say that I am cynical and traipse sadly around it picking things up and putting them back down again. French Connection's most hideous are bundled on a rack. I'm sure there is something marked Chanel, but it is so ashamed of itself that it has hidden amidst a rack of gaudy summer jackets so as not to be noticed.

The store's air conditioning is in overdrive and there are hot patches and freezing patches all over the floor we scramble around, picking up anything that is white, cream or vaguely festive looking. I am not confident, but I swipe a pink silver satin thing that has a halter neck or something off a rack. I like the fabric (I shop mostly by touch, and can often be found lurking around H&M picking things up and petting them like adorable domestic animals). It also has an eighty-dollar price tag, so what's to lose, why not?

Of course the fitting room is communal. Of course communal dressing rooms strike paralytic fear into me, all bras and socks and mirrors to the ceiling and cruel, unforgiving lighting. Of course the store is only moderately busy that day, but there are still people around who are partially naked, and I'm happy for them but don't intend to join them. I spin to Kathleen and mime a 'Nope nope nope,' and without batting an eyelid she turns to the attendant and calmly says, 'Excuse me? My friend here is trying on potential wedding dresses and it would be great if you could find us somewhere more private to try them on,' in a tone that at once threatens, 'I may or may not be carrying a concealed weapon', and flirts, 'Your hair looks really cute today'. She is all tenderness and spine.

I am not confident, nor do I feel particularly good, but I am shown a large fitting room off to the side of the half-naked-lady plaza. I try on something cornflower blue that gets stuck and remove myself from it, angry. I consider just walking out of the room and asking Kathleen does she want to go get a Bloody Mary somewhere. As I am thinking this I am halfway into the pink silver satin thing, and I am really surprised it fits me, like, really well, and I tie the halter neck and my face turns red.

I walk out of the dressing room all flushed and trying to keep tears from coming out of my eyes, and then Kathleen walks straight to me and puts her arms around me, pats my back and says, 'Yes, this is right, here's your dress,' and I'm sure a few of the half-naked women start applauding because this is the dress in which I'm going to get married.

Look, so many people cringe when I tell them we eloped to Disneyland. They make disgusted faces, as if my and CB's mutual love for Americana were something shameful. Why not the Redwoods, they ask. Lake Tahoe? You're in California, they say, there's so much beauty all around you, so much nature, so much romance, and you choose something so tacky, so fake, so corporate.

Yes we did, my overeducated, hipster, liberal comrades, and I will not flicker in the face of your judgement. We did not go ironically – we went with enthusiasm and wonder. We wanted to go on roller coasters and run around with costumed characters from our childhoods. We didn't just want to be away from San Francisco's constant posturing and posing: we wanted to be away from reality. We both needed a break. Not a scenic, quiet break but a stupid break. A break from adulthood. Yes, marrying each other was undoubtedly the most grown-up thing either of us has ever done, including moving five thousand miles away from home to start a new life. We wanted to look back on the first lines of this new chapter and feel the rush of excitement, the strange sensation of laughing from sheer joy. Growing up is for suckers. We might masquerade as adults with our worry lines, our grey hairs, his job and my endless search for one. The beginning of our marriage, the continuation of our life together, was not serene or picturesque because that is not how either of us operates, that is not where either of us finds happiness. It was a pinball machine, all lights, all noise, just for us. So people roll their eyes, like, Disneyland, like, how cliché, how shallow. That's OK. They weren't invited.

CB and I lie on the hotel bed, sleepy. Outside, in the pool, a thousand teenage bodies trill with laughter and splash. They are baby birds at a fountain. They are a noisy, cluttered, teenaged orchestra, away from home, who knows, maybe for the first time. They're distractingly loud but it's OK. Their splashing is a weird symphony: it sounds like freedom and newness. It is quiet by eleven.

I write detailed and consistent posts every day on Facebook about attending Bikram Yoga. I buy a month-long subscription for thirty dollars to a local studio that smells like death and feet and horror. I go ten times, ten days in a row. Three dollars a class. Ninety minutes, twenty-six poses, a hundred and five degrees with humidity. The vast mirrored room, which is usually packed with extremely tanned, flexible skinny people, has a sign on the door with 'Bikram's Torture Chamber' written above it.

I am not athletic. This is all very hard. I cry a lot, but nobody else in the class can tell because I am sweating so hard and am rose-pink from head to toe. But I keep going back, and I write a small note into the newsfeed every day about it. When I am telling my friends through the medium of the internet that today I didn't fall over, today I managed every pose, we're on day six now so day seven is tomorrow, I am trying to tell them that I am struggling with all of this running away, all of this solitude. I am trying to tell them I miss them, to direct their attention to me, to point out that something big is happening in my life. I am trying to tell them I am about to transform. When they comment on my posts and say, 'You can do it, you're doing great,' I am hearing them tell me that eloping is going to be just fine, I can do it, I'm doing great organizing all of this insanity alone, without my sister or my mother or my father or my friends.

I stand in the dense room day after day, and my mind leaves my body sometimes. I am so aware of every muscle that I have, their pulling and their growing. I am paler and larger than everyone else in the room, and I am the moon against their forest of lean, brown-bodied trees. I am waxing, not waning; I am full and I am rising.

I change my mind about the dress three days before the wedding and order a green floaty summer thing off the internet. I decide I will wear my gown for the ceremony then change into my floaty runaway dress for the wedding brunch and the flight to LAX. CB thinks I am a lunatic, his suit casual, mismatched, dapper, tells me he'd marry me in my pyjamas. I threaten him that I might just do that, much easier, much softer, much more like me than all this bloody fabric and circumstance. We do, in the end, elect to look even kind of like a bride and groom. We want something, even if it is only a tiny visual token, to remind us that what we are doing is of weight and of splendour.

We are unaccessorized and casual, so I make a tiny bouquet for each of us: one for his blazer and one for my hands, from mint paper and pearls and sprigs of lavender and baby's breath gifted to me by Katie who works in the florist's up in Noe Valley. I met her in Galway when I studied there – she was part of the writers' society I was secretary of. Back then, we'd written in dark apartments late and drunk in the same collective of mad folks, and naturally the earth moves in such a way that, of course, she's my local florist. Blonde curls and a clipped voice, she wraps the odd-ended sprigs in brown paper and wishes me luck.

In Anaheim, CB and I literally drop our bags on our bed and walk straight out of our room five minutes after we arrive. It is forty minutes until fireworks and I will be absolutely damned if our first dance is not under those nightly Disney musically co-ordinated multicoloured explosions (Bridezilla roars her last battle cry from somewhere deep within me). We are jittery and overexcited. We are en speedy route to the lift back down when we encounter our first clutch of cheerleaders, three girls walking in an arrow formation down the hallway with furious determination. They all wear shorts and their legs are honey-wood-stained, flawless. We walk past them and they stop at a door. The girl at the point of their arrow hammers on it aggressively. CB and I keep walking, but as we wait for the elevator we are stage left of their melodrama.

The door they stand in front of creaks open, just a crack.

'Are you fucking serious?' hisses the apparent alpha. 'I cannot fucking believe you.'

I can hear the lift approaching, but don't want it to get here.

The alpha raises her voice. 'You're really doing this? Is this what is happening right now?'

CB and I lock eyes – he puts his hand over his mouth in mock horror. The elevator arrives and the doors slowly open. The alpha raises her voice again.

'You are fucking gross. I cannot believe you are ditching us to have sex. I am so done with you.'

We walk into the elevator and the doors start to close.

'You are SO GROSS –'

We are moving downward and away from their débâcle. I tell CB I'm so glad we're not teenagers any more, and he replies, 'Yeah, but nobody can swear like they can.' He's right. They really mean it.

The cart does not move for maybe ten minutes. We are starting to get a little uncomfortable; the humour of the situation has worn off. Being stranded in the intestine of an indoor roller coaster is funny for three or four minutes, but when the time gets longer you have plenty of opportunity to wonder how you're going to get out, if something is going to happen suddenly, if something is going to snap or crack or start sparking all wrong.

Moving at an insanely fast pace in the sparkling darkness is fine, you know. It is a rush and you are breathless because you can't help it; it is not a journey to be taken stony faced. But grinding to a halt and cold, clinical brightness revealing the mechanics of the magic is nothing short of frightening. There is a smugness that comes with having seen a glimpse of the man behind the curtain, the truth behind the smoke and mirrors, the aspiring actor in the Donald Duck costume, sure. But then you know you can't undo that truth, and the longer you look, the less of a child you become.

I do not want to disembark our little imaginary spaceship and be quietly escorted out the emergency exit. I want this never to have happened; I want CB and me to continue our speedy flight through the galaxy and never have to look at the spine of it, the mechanical lungs of it. I do not want to know anything about reality, not now, not tonight.

As I am becoming panicky and indignant, a boyish voice tells us over some invisible intercom that we'll be resuming space travel in twelve, eleven, ten – and I am relieved, but assume we'll be hand-held through the end of the ride, sluggishly dragged back to the boarding gate.

I am wrong.

We start at the speed at which we left, and CB and I scream from the velocity, the scream turns into laughter and we can see everything, all the grey steel limbs, all the other little rockets, every vertebra of the track we are ripping along, everything is so visible, so bright, so terrifying and joyous. There is no going back, and we ascend the final tunnel for the final drop before the end and I love this, all this truth, this searing reality. We lift our hands again from the safety bar and raise them above our heads, waiting for the bright drop, eyes open, eating it all in.

Other Irish People or *The Tarot* or *The World*

*L*ook, I didn't come to America to meet Irish people. I know that's a thing people do – you know, emigrate then nestle into an Irish community. I understand that – in fact, I think it's an absolutely great idea, the tribes of diaspora here are so, so welcoming. I was tempted all right, don't get me wrong, but I held off.

I know a lot of Irish people already, for obvious reasons. I left Ireland to see the world, and that world includes unknowable multitudes of different kinds of people. I wanted to meet people who aren't just like me; by this, I mean people whose stories aren't set in the same backdrop or spoken in the same dialect as mine. I wanted to make friends with these new people, and I knew that would be hard, and I knew that would be alienating and often extremely frustrating, and there would be a million dead ends before there would be laughter, but that was the choice I made. I chose this because I felt it would scare me and crystallize me into something more resilient. I chose this because I was hungry for new experience, new stories, new perspectives, and now here we are cusping on the second summer, and it was worthwhile because I am different now, I have grown a little more, and that is what I wanted. It was hard and I was lonely and I complained, but here's the thing: growing is hard. Change is hard. And that's OK. Eventually, I met writers and artists of all sorts and they are becoming friends now, my splintered American family.

Every so often, though, I am led to Irish people. Something happens, someone I know is here, somebody's accent in a bar lifts my attention and I am amongst my own again. Some of them have been here for a long time; some of them arrived in similar situations to mine. One phone call, one-way flight, one gigantic, reality-bending change and they're here. Keep in mind, too, I moved here with an Irish guy, and proposed to him, and married him. I wake up next to him and go asleep next to him. We live together, like. In the same tiny apartment. So realistically I get a fair healthy dose of talking about King Crisps and laughing at *Father Ted* and hissing angrily about current affairs from someone who comes from the same city as me – the touchstones I miss are often there in the hands of my partner.

When I meet other Irish people, or people who have spent a long time in my country, something always comes over me no matter how different I am to that person. A warmth, a sense of calm, a relief. Maybe this effect is only apparent because almost all of the people I spend my time with are American, and the freshness and familiarity of another Irish person's voice is an open window in a sometimes suffocating environment. There is a lot about us that is nothing like them, and sometimes that is just what I need.

As time passed I stopped counting people who were born on our soil as Irish. The word Irish changed in meaning for me. People who lived there, people whose parents are there, people who spent twenty years there twenty years ago. The span of our people is uncanny.

So here's the thing about tarot cards. There are seventy-eight cards in a usual deck with different representations and meanings, containing different truths and possibilities. Bits of stories, that's what they are. I've been reading them since I was around fifteen, on and off. It's not like I think they can actually tell the future. I'm far too cynical for that. It's more that I like what happens when you sit down with them, how life can suddenly be simplified into seventy-eight fragments, and when drawn at random they can give sudden and remarkable perspective. The stories are universal, and can be read in such a way that they connect all of human experience: grief, change, growth. Here. Let me show you. Let me tell you about some cards I drew at random. Let me tell you about the random nature of human connection. Let me tell you about some of the Irish people I met.

The Two of Cups
or

Overflowing
or

Empaths in the Water

The Two of Cups can be traditionally read as a friendship or relationship built on confidence. Two people have been looking for something: they find it in one another. Both become newly capable of understanding each other. Something begins.

The pool is the kind of shocking blue that doesn't ever occur in nature and we are up to our bellies in it, somewhere outside the city, basking in Sunnyvale's evening heat. Every so often a Caltrain screams by, all speeding importance, and breaks our conversation with its charging wail. We pause for it, like the angelus or something. Jenn used to work in the coffee shop at the end of the street CB and I lived on and now we're standing in a pool in swimming togs with our hair clipped up talking about our feelings. Look, there's that thing about the wing of the butterfly and the hurricane again, a face you kind of know from your street suddenly appearing on the other side of the world as a new friend, a message in an inbox, a meeting at a party – this is just how the world works and I don't question it any more: I just marvel at it. Her boyfriend, Matthew, works for the same company as CB, their story parallel with ours.

One day, almost suddenly, here they were, in the California wilds, far from the city. She works from home for an international coffee association. She is from Maryland but has lived in Ireland so long that her accent is familiar and clear.

We stand there in the last sunshine of the day, the shadow of the beautiful apartment complex creeping across the water, darkening it. We move from the middle of the rectangle towards the last feet of light, eventually to the last corner where the sun is still tenderly heating the water. We aren't even really swimming, just kind of standing, stretching, moving our arms in the antigravity of it. This is the kind of water I like, controlled and clean and limited. I tell her about my water dreams. We talk, for a brief time, about frightening things that have happened to us. Revealing conversations are something I thought I'd kind of outgrown. I'm not a big fan of surprise confessionals usually. I'm very, well, here are my cards – see how close to my chest they are. We don't know each other well but I guess it just comes out. We talk about how weird California is, how weird Californians are. It feels better to know that someone else gets it. Neither of us has offices or workplaces to go to any more.

This week, though, things changed for her. She has gotten a job with the same internet goliath CB and Matthew work for. I am so excited for her and can't stop telling her that – I tell her that as soon as I can I'll be trying to get one there too, trying to go be a responsible adult, kind of. We stand in the pool and pull lazy yoga poses. The tree, kind of. The bow, kind of. I envision a world where I have somewhere to go in the morning, where I have a regular pay cheque. Jenn is an ethnomusicologist and a maverick barista, but will be working as a PA. I want to be a PA.

'There's something so exciting about going to a place every day where you have something to do, where there'll be lots of other people,' she says. Noise. Conversation. I know exactly how she feels.

Earlier in the year, in the first few weeks after she and Matthew had landed, we went for quiet afternoon drinks in a small restaurant on the top floor of the Westfield Mall. It was a sort of blind-friend-date. Half blind. We'd met before, in a different world, in the hodgepodge of the Twisted Pepper's daytime façade on Abbey Street. We've all these friends in common, we paced the same streets and moved in the same circles for so long without ever really stopping and saying, hey, how's it going, let's, like, shake hands or hug or something. That's pure Dublin, mind you, the casual acknowledgement without any need to introduce yourself – any time I had broken it in the past I was met with surprise or annoyance, the 'I'm Sarah, by the way' bringing forth an 'I … know?' Jenn and I had first formally met at a small party in an apartment in Mountain View and had sat with other tender Irish people in a hot tub drinking wine out of big plastic cups. I asked her to let me know if she was ever in the city. She did, on a Wednesday, and I rushed to her, unselfconsciously.

We'd met in the mall because it is the most neutral landmark for someone who doesn't know the city, a huge, looming obviousness, right next to the train station. We sat over cocktails with flowers in them, violet-grey concoctions, and got slightly day drunk. She was about to get her mad curly hair cut off and needed liquid courage. We talked then about how we missed Henry Street in the rain, everyday channels through the city, streets walked so regularly they were veins really through a body that might as well be hers or mine. Ducking into the shining, white-grey atrium of the Jervis Centre, rooting through clothes shops until the wet stopped. We lament the shops we left behind. The ordinary.

When our drinks are finished, I tell her to come with me, just for a sec, before she goes. I am uncertain if she's going to think what I'm about to do is weird, if it will sever the first threads of understanding we have just woven over our drinks, if it will restore us to nods and half waves and acquaintanceship. We walk up flights of winding escalators until we hit the very top floor of Nordstrom, the department store. In the furthest corner there is a tiny concession, smaller than my apartment but with a sign that feels like five thousand miles away.

Topshop. 'Yeah, I know,' I say to Jenn, who is laughing, it isn't Jervis Street or anything, but it's familiar, at least, that weird corner high-street expensive staple next to Marks & Spencer and Boots in the Jervis Centre that sometimes you'd just walk into to walk into and pick things up and put things down – feels like Dublin for a moment. Definitely doesn't feel like California. We hug, walk around, buy nothing but feel better.

When we eventually get out of the swimming pool, much later in the year, we sit on sun-chairs wrapped in towels and I think we are both glad we talked about sad, difficult things in the water. I feel far less alone than I had that morning, and I don't think I will feel alone again for a long while. Strange what one conversation can do.

Later in the evening Jess will come over from her nook in Mountain View. I have tarot cards in my handbag, but we are too busy talking for me to give them a reading. We will get intensely involved in a conversation where we unselfconsciously talk about our personal recipes for different kinds of potatoes. We will mourn Grafton Street, mourn Henry Street, mourn the rain – but we mourn together.

The Page of Wands
or

Awe
or

Three Irish People in the California Academy of Science
The Page of Wands is often read as a symbol of something begun in the past that has finally blossomed or come to

fruition. It can signify achievement, ambition, new adventure.
It also can connote childlike awe and wonder.

In the butterfly dome in the centre of the vast
museum in the centre of Golden Gate Park, the
three of us wander slowly around, in awe, trying to
snap pictures of the paper-winged creatures around
us. The place is alive with them and I find myself
very moved, wishing that one, by some magical,
photogenic accident, would land on my nose or in
my hair. Jess and Stephen have brought me with
them – they have yearly memberships – and today
I am a five-year-old and they are like my cool aunt
and uncle and this is some wonderful, fascinating
day trip. I have not done something like this in a
long time.

Jess and I met on another blind-friend-date in the
autumn just gone, at a concert in the Fillmore, some
punk rock cabaret superstar and her band. We drank
a lot of wine extremely quickly and talked a lot and
I'm pretty sure spent a fair deal of time weeping about
being far away from our families, our mothers (here is
another Two of Cups – here is our emotion, here is our
wine, here are our hearts, here is the beginning). Her
fiancé, Stephen, is from Beaumont; she's from Tallaght.
She is blonde, sunshine warm and has a penny-gap in
her smile. He is tall and brown eyed. Their accents are
medicine.

So some spring day we are in the butterfly dome
looking at these little creatures of flight. A sloping

passageway winds up from the ground-floor entrance around this jungle in a box until it hits the top-floor exit. From inside there we can see all of the museum; the walls are made of glass. We move in a slow tide of people. It is unusually hot, to keep the winged things alive. We had to pass through an airlock to get in, entering in little groups of ten or twelve. There are signs that say be careful, we might have to check your clothes on the way out, these little guys are clever. They will stow away in the folds of your sleeves, your hair, your scarf. Clever, reckless, ambitious creatures with a three-day lifespan.

As we ascend I notice that down in the bowels of the jungle room there are failed escapees, emperor blue, throwing themselves up against the glass, set us free, set us free. Some lie like tissue all broken at the very bottom but, God, at least they tried. Some are so exhausted that their movement is slow and drunken but they bat themselves against the glass. Freedom, freedom, freedom. We will not settle for what you have handed us. We want out. We can see through this wall, we can see a whole world out there and we will try until our wings fold to get out – and one by one the wings fold, and one by one more join the barricade.

I think a lot about luck, and escape, and the weirdness of being in a museum in a new city with two people who grew up less than an hour away from where I grew up. When we leave the dome they put us through the airlock again. When we walk outside, back into the cool of the museum, we are the ones who got out, the butterflies still struggling against the glass.

The Star
or

The Future
or

Bread
The Star is, quite literally, a light on the horizon. In a reading it suggests a good omen, infinite possibilities, hope.

Jaimie brings soda bread to the Superbowl party. Her mother made it – both of her parents are from Sligo and have been living in SF a long time. We met in a basement speakeasy, early on in my time here. I read a poem along with a jazz band about being a teacher and she rushed up to me and said, 'Ohmygod are you Irish?' And I said 'Yes,' and she said so was she and that she was a teacher too. Her parents were Irish. She was in the Rose of Tralee one year. Her accent is full Sligo, zero San Francisco. She teaches English in Juvenile Detention. She is slender and enthusiastic; she has a tiny, shining nose-ring.

She tells me, in the garden of her boyfriend's house while the football game is on, about how complicated it is being first generation, of having a split identity. I am so excited about the conversation that I do not even remember to take a single slice of soda bread. This bread is not a thing they make here. It only comes from Irish hands. I don't remember who won the game that night – I'm pretty sure San Francisco lost. Beyoncé was beautiful at the half-time show, a queen, always. On the tram home I think a lot about what would happen if CB and I started a family in America, about how complicated it seems to be, being of a first generation. Jaimie understood those complications, somehow, and navigated them with grace. Some of us, some of them, a diamond in the side of her nose glinting in the light of the game. I think about how the bread must have been wonderful, how it had been made by Irish hands. I can taste it as we go into the night.

The Knight of Swords
or

The Field
or

Ten Years

Cards in the house of Swords are usually warnings, all but the Knight. He points to travel. He points to pursuit. He points to chasing and capturing your dreams. The Knight does not wait for the world to come to him: he goes and conquers the world.

Ger and Christine come down from LA for a few days and CB and I catch them for a pint on their last night in the city. We bar crawl slowly down Valencia Street.

Ger and I go way back. We met when we were fifteen or something, stood around the same suburban green, went on to work in the same cinema. Always moved in the same circle as time passed, then, look, somehow we were both in California – who'd have known we'd end up this far gone?

As we drink, on more than one occasion we say to each other, 'Jesus, it's a long way from Edenmore, it's a long way from Coolock.' Ger is tall, a graphic designer now. I think he was always tall, but it's hard to remember because we were only kids when we met. He has a beard and a mischief face, is handsome. Christine is a yoga instructor from Clondalkin. She is really elegant and earnest and I am immediately sad that she lives so far away because I feel like we probably could have been friends. She tells me about how kind Americans have been to her, how she thinks the Irish could learn a thing or two from them. She's right. We throw the pints into us.

We talk about how lads on BMX bikes used to shoot at Ger and the lads with pellet guns as they walked from their suburb down to mine. We wonder if they're still in Dublin, those boys with the fake guns. Ger shakes his head, says he was proud of his New Rock boots, that they differentiated him from them. I remember those boots. Huge, sturdy leather things. He says his ma gave them to charity after he moved out of home. We guess where they might be, probably still the same: those things are built to last an eternity.

When he first came to LA, Ger posed as Braveheart on Hollywood Boulevard for a while, for photo opportunities and tips, all painted blue with wild hair and a kilt. I think this is epic and perfect. He lived in New Zealand before here. He tells me how all the lads from when we were younger are doing. Some of them have kids; most of them are living abroad.

We sit in Gestalt on 16th Street until we are kicked out and the lights are turned on. We walk up Valencia to hail them a cab. We're swaying and laughing and I think how hard it is to be this relaxed with Americans, how grateful I am for this evening. Ger goes, 'I can't believe you're married.' I go, 'Neither can I.' We go, 'It's a long way from Coolock.'

At one point Ger and I hug and he says he's proud of me. I have tears in my eyes and I tell him I'm proud of him, and I could not humanly mean it more than I do in that moment. We are not children in the field. We are adults in the world. Maybe it's the drink, but I am so overcome. This is so far from home; this is so good.

Two Letters

I give Sam back his shirt in a dark café on 24ᵗʰ Street. It has been waiting for him in my apartment since the night that he and Tim walked me home from the BART station after the Berkeley Poetry Slam, that week when CB was in Seattle and I was alone. The two American boys and I sat up. We sat up late and read poems to each other over and over in different voices and at different speeds. We drank a bottle of wine and all the whiskey that was in the house. Moriarty's fur made Tim's eyes and nose run. How worried I was, at the train station in the dark, asking them would they come and keep me company. How huge the looming 'No' had been, how it threatened a crushing rejection, how friendship is such a slow game. Just two letters, I always told myself as I asked hard questions. 'No' is just two letters, and the yes is worth that risk.

I thought as I handed the denim thing back to Sam how grateful I was for that night. For two big, strong poet lads escorting me to my empty house in the late dark, for drinking with me and telling me poems until

I was so happy and drunk that I wasn't scared of the noises our apartment block made, of the fire escape that led from the wild street to my bedroom's sliding doors, of the temporary coldness of CB's side of the bed and how the starfish stretch I could make in the centre of the bed just wasn't worth his absence. Their yes had been the unfolding petals of a new story and the seeded promise of stories to come. This was what made me realize my home was no longer empty – this city was no longer empty.

When I was packing up our little flat near Love Lane and the Grand Canal in Dublin, exactly a year from this moment in the café in 24th Street in the belly of the Mission, I sat with my parents and wept amongst the packing cases and bags. Everything I was throwing away, donating, gifting to friends so I could reduce my possessions to what I was permitted to take on my flight with me – every single thing was a story; was someone's face, was a hangover, was a hoarse throat from singing Julie Andrews songs on Harcourt Street in the rain at two in the morning. 'Take care of that lasagne dish, won't you? It came free with a pack of Dolmio pasta sauce but one time me and Christina made the most delicious bacon macaroni-and-cheese tomato thing inside of it and the breadcrumbs, oh, the breadcrumbs we used were mouldy and we didn't realize until it had been cooked and how our hearts broke but jaws ached from laughter and I'm pretty sure we ate it anyway, so please, take care of the dish, won't you? Don't break it or sell it, I'll be back for it –'

I would say things exactly like this, in earnest, to the tribe I moved through Dublin with, as I gifted them my clothes and kitchenware, hoping secretly they'd be used and lived with as opposed to being kept in dusty wardrobes and cabinets. Sometimes on the internet I see photographs and recognize a dress or cardigan of mine wrapped around someone I love, and in that moment my emigrant-ghost arms are around them tightly. There was a story with every single thing that I passed on. Until all that was left was enough for two suitcases and a backpack. Just like that, pursed lips blowing the dandelion of my life in Ireland and scattering my stories to the homes of people I love, with the half-promise that I'd be home, some day, looking for that dress to wear to Doyle's, or Sweeney's, or Grogan's, or whatever monstrosities spring up in their place in the Dublin that has not been born yet. But half-promises is all those things were – I will not be coming home to collect these things I gave away. I know that fully now. Those stories belong to my friends now.

The apartment CB and I moved into here in America was so empty for so long. I took this emptiness into the streets of the city with me every time I left the house. Such a complicated and beautiful place, the Bay. San Francisco is a girl in her grandmother's clothes: young, but with the trappings of a woman three times her age. A child dragged up as an old lady. I could not see, a year ago, how like me she is – I was too busy treating her like a paper doll. A pop-up book. I could admire the things I saw here, sure, but I had no stories based in these hills to tell or to survive on. There were no words in this beautiful new book yet. All I had was nostalgia, oh, back in Dublin, at home in Dublin, when I lived in Dublin, I used to live in Dublin and –

Eventually, as the months drew past, new stories began to emerge. I listened to the stories new people I met told me. I made stories by myself in the city; I made stories with CB. Eventually, somehow, I became so busy gathering new stories that I forgot to keep counting the days until the emptiness of my new home became fullness instead. All at once the warm blush of spring was at my window and my freckles were emerging again from wherever they hide during the wintertime. Moriarty had become, suddenly, a huge, monstrous tom cat while I wasn't even looking.

I checked my journal this morning – the first of May is on the next page; April had stacked its dates quietly. The numbers of days, or weeks, or months are no longer the first thing to flash across my mind when I wake up in the morning. The first of May is my one-year anniversary in San Francisco and I had been desperate for it to arrive, because I had believed that with its arrival I would have finally gained a sense of home. A sense of peace.

I would love to say that these were the only reasons why I had obsessed over the first of May, but there was one other thing. When I booked my visa package in the big offices on the quays by the Liffey, it came with a return flight. SFO to Heathrow to Dublin – May first.

This was deliberate, exactly 365 days after my arrival. I would secretly, some days, dream of this flight. It was non-refundable; it was a sure bet. It was an excuse to leave: my visa is up and here is a seat on a plane to take me to my family or to a new life in London. It was the gleaming green exit sign, the four letters that would lead me away if things had not gotten better by the rise of the second summer. I had told myself again and again, if you don't have a job in a fancy tech company in Silicon Valley, if you are still broke, if the challenge of emigration breaks your relationship instead of making it – the door will open on the first of May and you can go again.

There will be an empty seat on that flight, that secret of mine. The seat will not contain a broken-hearted Irish ex-patriot who gave up and fled home. Maybe they will call my name out over the intercom. Maybe some sleepy traveller will use the extra space to rest their head, or their legs, or get to see the two sunsets that happen on the fourteen-hour journey across the ocean – but it won't be me. I am not afraid any more of not knowing when I will feel the cold breath of Dublin again. Maybe this coming winter, maybe next spring. But it won't be next week. That seat will just be an empty space instead.

There is little to no empty space in my and CB's little house now. There is cat hair everywhere, a bookshelf, an altar, thrifted cheap furniture, a nine-dollar typewriter, a globe. There are echoes of birthday parties, brainstorming sessions, screenings of *The*

Snapper late at night, Dungeons and Dragons and too many mimosas.

This is the sofa I lay on after the boat accident at Alcatraz. This is where the blonde hairdresser braided my hair the morning of my wedding. This is the coffee table CB and I carried up the hill together. This is the statue of a unicorn I bought the day I got the Silicon Valley job I wasn't allowed to take because it broke my visa restrictions. This is the scorecard from the first poetry slam I won here. These new stories and memories bleed down the steps and into the streets of this city, out into Noe Valley and the Castro and the Haight and Downtown and out into Oakland and further to Berkeley. Finally, stories. It took a year. A whole, solid year – and there are still stories to be had. I am still hungry for the myths of San Francisco, I have still so much to do. There is still the occasional, thundering dark 'No' on the horizon. But there is still a world full of yes.

I would not spoil the ending for the girl giving away her artefacts and being held by her father as she said goodbye to her life in Ireland. I would just say this:

Don't be afraid of the word no. It's just two letters.

Don't be afraid of the word go. It's just two letters.

Postscript

Scenes and Notes from a Road Trip (San Francisco, CA–Portland, OR)

*I*t takes us forever to break from San Francisco, from Oakland, from the wider Bay Area, the traffic so slow as if it were the Bay itself saying, no, don't leave, never leave, stay here and do nothing else, we have everything you need here. Still, we drag ourselves up the freeway until the slew of fellow escapees in their cars loosens to an unknowable stretch of road. Nate says let's put on some tunes. Let's go around the car and make a playlist of guilty pleasures.

There is a tape deck in the minivan with a magic tape that has a wire that plugs into the headphone jack on a phone or mp3 player. CB, Amanda and I begin to type in our confessions. The four of us are all new friends, really. The road trip had been an idea dropped onto a bar table and we spun it and said, OK, let's go. Portland? Portland. We weren't sure of the length of the drive when we decided to do it. We never would have guessed that it would be eleven hours there and eleven hours back. The West Coast is a far longer wind than we'd imagined – maybe that would have discouraged us then, but with the stretch facing ahead of us as the first song bursts out of the old speakers in the van, we know we'll be able for it. It is almost seven in the evening and the sky is turning tender before night.

The road is lined with huge slices of burned rubber, like pencil shavings but huge and black, shed from the slow, heaving trucks and their fat tyres. Each slice is a burst tyre, the ghost of an accident, curling into a charred spiral. I take an anti-nauseant, which proceeds to make me a very special kind of sleepy and stupid.

There are sunflower fields, for hours. Thousands of lanky, summertime-looking blooms facing the sinking day and we are undeterred by the tiny dent we have placed in our journey because we have all these nineties hits to fuel us, this strange feeling of celebration emanating from all of them. Maybe it's because we were all only kids when these songs came out – these were the first songs to follow us on airwaves and in large foam headphones attached to rickety Walkmans. We discover as we thunder down the freeway that not only are we all linked by these beats but we all, all four of us, came into the world via caesarean section. We are all the eldest of our families.

Nate is a writer and tutor and Amanda is a film producer and barista. He has glasses and a moustache and she has glasses and this inky mane of hair with a widow's peak and the subtlest natural grey streak right at the front. They are distinctly un-California, as cynical as CB and I are to ourselves but can't really be in public. Risking a road trip with new friends could wind up with nobody ever speaking to each other again or awkwardness arising like an elephant between all of us that none of us will point out – but it doesn't feel like that. Even when the car goes quiet between conversations it's fine, just chill, just comfortable, just like extended journeys in confined spaces should be when they are pretty much ideal.

We stop to get coffee and use the jacks in a Burger King somewhere. When we open the door of the car the heat is dense and thick and we exclaim at it, so unexpected. The tar of the parking lot must have absorbed the heat of the day, Amanda says. She and Nate are from Virginia, so this is not the first time they have felt this heat, but it makes me almost dizzy. CB smokes a cigarette and I gape at him, like how can you put smoke in your body when it is so hot that we are almost smoke ourselves?

Amanda gets a fifty-cent ice-cream and I steal some of it with a plastic spoon. Soft serve in heat like this is weird and tastes like those nineties songs sound: like being a small kid and being excited about everything.

Nate and CB talk to each other like old-timey southern gentlemen as we walk back to the van.

'I do declare, this weather is not appropriate for my sartorial choices –'

'I do declare –'

'I do declare –' and they are just laughing at each other.

Friendship budding in front of your eyes is a wonderful and unusual thing.

Night comes on strong and the road is black. The trucks are like huge, dumb, speeding giants all glaring at us with their lights, so much bigger than we are. We don't know it yet but we're coming up on the redwoods – it is too dark to see a damn thing out there. It's been a while since our last stop so we pull into a roadside town called Shasta to look for food. None of us is sure how midnight showed up so fast, but we are starving, even though we have eaten so many chips and pretzel pieces, and all of the hundreds of fast-food giants in this lot are closed except Wendy's. I have never eaten Wendy's and don't know what they sell – burgers and stuff, seemingly, nothing exciting. Their insignia is the face of a child, a girl with red hair and pigtails and freckles staring past you into the ether. CB orders something called Son of the Baconator and we all cackle and I tell him he's going to get food poisoning, but he orders it anyway and I secretly am jealous of all the bacon he's going to get to eat and I think he is very brave. I am sort of afraid of fast food so I eat around three heavily salted fries but drink around a gallon of soda-fountain Coke as we sit in the empty, huge car park, doors of the van flung open. We are hyperactive for a moment from all the chemicals, maybe too from the weirdness of sitting in a car park in a town called Shasta eating burgers at midnight with no idea where we'll be sleeping or if we'll be sleeping or how long it'll really take to get to Oregon, to Portland.

I lie across the third row of seats and close my eyes. The boys sit up front. Amanda is lying across the middle row. We are snoozing in the dark and they are listening to Bruce Springsteen and re-casting *Star Trek: The Next Generation* with Bill Murray and Anjelica Huston. I am half listening to their casting decisions, but there is a speaker right beside my head so Springsteen is reverberating through me as we roar through the night. I've never really been into him, not really at all; the sound of him is the dull static of other people's music choices in the endless stream of retail jobs I worked before the recession. I never really understood other people's worship of him, their reverence at this 'Boss' of theirs – I got nothing from him; but now in this speeding darkness I start to understand what it maybe is like to be born to run, maybe we all really were. I am half asleep and I am this song in the moment, sort of transcending all the discomfort of the back seat and my too-long legs, I'm just that progression, just that dun-dun-dun, baby we were born to runnnnn – and I feel suddenly epic, like all of us are epic for doing this adventure together, like all of the choices that led up to this moment were in anticipation of this, this, this.

We go a little further then stop at a rest stop, and CB isn't sick from Wendy's but Nate kind of is. Considering he's the only one with a full licence we figure we should go back and crash at a Holiday Inn somewhere. I take a photo of them talking to each other, and they look like they're older than they are but not, like, they look like they're in their thirties or forties: in a way that the photograph looks like it was taken a long time ago. We are already in the Redwoods but not quite in Oregon – we're maybe two hours off breaking out of California. We turn around and hit the nearest hotel. The late-night-reception girl squints at CB's passport and questions his nationality. 'You don't sound Irish.' I fume and look silently at Amanda, who gives me a comforting eye-roll.

Our room is enormous. Two full double beds, one TV. It's actually pretty nice for a roadside trucker den. We don't talk much, just collapse in the heat onto the cool white linen. I don't sleep, not exactly, more flicker between rest and alertness. I hate the heat: it does sick things to my skin and makes me want to throw up, always has. So I lie there, and sometimes I am lucid dreaming and sometimes I am gone, and sometimes I am staring at the red dot of the standby on the huge television screen. In the morning we eat from the all-you-can-eat continental largely reheated via microwave deep-fried breakfast buffet, at like seven. I nurse a yogurt and a pretty sad-looking banana; CB makes a waffle with batter and a waffle iron. It looks perfect when it is done, like a cartoon, like an illustration of an American breakfast waffle. Amanda is back in the room taking a shower and Nate, CB and I eat quietly, sleepy headed.

Someone in the bathroom near the small dining area is getting loudly and violently unwell. It is alarming and slightly theatrical. We wonder if he is dying in there. I notice that Nate has a tattoo on his arm of a line, like a thick, deliberate graph on his skin, and I ask what it is. He tells me it's the narrative arc. I don't tell him how cool I think that is. I just say, 'Cool,' and continue to eat my weird peach yoghurt.

Two hours evaporate quickly and we hit the state line and cheer our exit. I'm kind of stupid again from anti-nauseants and snooze in the front seat. Nate puts on a podcast, and we listen and it's pretty funny and we chuckle along, and I am really good at snoozing sitting up, so comfortable until everyone loudly and suddenly recoils from something they see on the side of the road and I open my eyes just in time, just in time to see a flash of it – a huge, ripped thing pushed to the side of the road, and I think it is a human just for a moment because it is so big and so broken. Amanda points out that it must be a deer, but I can't unsee the human in the carcass, but now we're two miles past it and the road is winding a downward spiral into a valley of huge, towering trees. There is a crucifix on the roadside covered in ancient flowers, and it is gone in a moment and I let my eyelids get heavy again.

Seven Feathers Casino looms on the left horizon. We wonder aloud all four of us if we are passing through Native land, and for a moment I feel like it's pretty cool that we're crossing land that still belongs to folks who came from America before White America, then I am suddenly ashamed and sad. Colonial theory was beat through my hungover head all the way through college, and I sometimes wonder how close a miss Ireland had from something like this, if we even had a miss at all. We pass the enormous, full-colour statue of a great American eagle swooping down into the fountain outside the hotel lobby, an unmoving statue of a trout the length of a car clenched between the bird's greedy, sharp claws.

We stop at a gas station called Love's. The sign is canary yellow and the logo is red, orange and pink. It shares aesthetic structure with what I'd imagine a 1970s Car Wash Barbie playset would look like. A lot of my doll accessories when I was a small kid were from my mam's or aunties' childhoods, and I loved them. One in particular was a bright yellow-and-white Vespa, perfect Barbie size. As we roll up to Love's I feel like if I look carefully enough a life-size incarnation of that little scooter would be waiting for me somewhere. I snap a picture of the sign.

When we are back on the road we see our first hitch-hikers. They have sunburnt calves and a wide-brimmed hat and walk by the side of the freeway. We don't contemplate aloud picking them up, none of us. But we notice them all the same.

CB is driving now. He has only had three lessons altogether, but has his permit and it isn't illegal as long as there's a licensed driver in the car. I am bolt upright, terrified of him driving, but the road is steady-ish, curving through more redwoods and Douglas firs and coiling and coiling onward. He does pretty well, only swerves once and it isn't even the most terrifying thing that's ever happened to me in a car. A shack with corrugated iron for walls stands on a grassier knoll on the roadside. The word 'HISTORY' is scrawled there, capitalized in skinny, white, spray-can letters. The paint has run, like it rained the night it was thrown up there by whoever wanted us to see that word, whoever wanted us to wonder about it. The letters are as tall as me, but it is painted askew so it is sort of tragic looking. It feels like a warning. I think about the roadkill again and watch CB's hands on the wheel.

The car beside us is marked with a long white bumper sticker, which reads in clear, professional black lettering: 'First Response Paranormal Investigation Team'. It is driven by a girl around our age, around her mid-twenties. She has a shoulder tattoo and a nose-ring. I can see them from where I am. Her hair is somewhere between mouse-brown and gold and is long and casually littered with braids. She wears huge aviator sunglasses, mirrored in the front. I wonder how many aliens she has seen, how many ghosts she has touched, or if she's just borrowed her mom's Prius for the day, if her own car has a 'My Mother Is a Paranormal Investigator' bumper sticker.

When we reach Portland I am unsure what to expect. Seemingly our apartment is in a suburb, and we roll about for a bit looking for it, away from the city. I realize I know nothing about our destination, other than vague details from the sketch show (*Portlandia*) that both affectionately and mercilessly pokes fun at the fact that young people go to Portland to retire. I had searched and compiled a short to-do list for our microscopic stay, which included buying doughnuts at the seemingly legendary Voodoo Donuts and seeing the inside of Powell's Books, a West Coast landmark. Other than that, my sister wanted a pair of socks from a fancy sock shop and I wanted to visit a couple of zine distros. Amanda has carefully shortlisted karaoke spots for the evening. Our eleven-hour trip there had not been to go sightseeing or fitting in fifty ridiculous tourist-ops in a day. It had been for those hours on the road. Those trees. Those weird things on the side of the road. Portland is just a turning point really, somewhere to hang out and take it easy for the oncoming evening and following day before the ride home.

Our sub-let is in the basement of a mansion. I am not exaggerating. We pull into a nook of a suburb a couple of miles from the city centre and the houses are the colour of teacakes and beautifully, beautifully designed. Toylike, almost, but more tasteful. I am immediately furious that I don't live here. The dude whose mom owns the place lets us into the basement apartment down the winding stairway behind the house, and I just about conceal my enormous adoration of the place while waiting for him to leave. It is like an apartment that looked so good in the early nineties that the owner never felt the need to change a thing about it as twenty years passed.

It reminds me intensely of visiting a friend's house as a kid and being amazed by how like your house it is but also how staggeringly unalike in the weird details, the paintings, the books on the shelf.

We drop our stuff and sit around for a moment then head out for food and booze. It is the fourth of July, so lots of places are closed and the streets are weirdly sparse. We walk through the neighbourhoods and eat barbeque at somewhere divey, nondescript and delicious enough to settle Nate's self-titled 'Dad' instincts, which pushed him to find the best place to eat as opposed to the first place to eat. We talk a bit about turning into our parents, but not in the same tone that we would have if we were teenagers or even if we were earlier on in our twenties. With this weird reverence, this, 'yeah that's pretty cool that it's happening' kind of tone. As if our parents are finally something to wholeheartedly respect as opposed to actively rebel against. Maybe this is a side-effect of reluctant adulthood, this subtle creeping adoration for the parents we no longer live with. We have a drink in a different bar and some topless guy shoots fireworks from his hands on the street outside. We sit in a weird smoking gazebo listening to affected hipsters in sunglasses complain about how illegal it is that people are setting off fireworks in the street. Amanda and Nate discuss the possibility that there are some people in the world who just hate fun.

As we walk through a small residential district somewhere around the Central East Side, the sun is setting again and it's mad to think how long it took to get here. It feels a bit like we're walking through a forest that just so happens to have houses in it. Cyclists pass, but the streets are quiet. Everyone is waiting for the big fireworks display downtown, or so the nice waiter at the barbeque place told us. We don't say much as we all walk through the little district, or if the others were talking I was tuned out because I was sort of emotionally overwhelmed by the place. It was so green. Like, greener than any housing estate I'd ever walked through even in the nicest parts of Dublin, even in Galway.

There are parties going on in the unpainted picket-fence backyards of the houses and on the lawns out front. The houses look like something my mother would have made from a kit ordered from a catalogue or bought from a craft fair when I was a kid, their sloping roofs and wooden exteriors, their wooden porches with little rocking chairs and unseasonal fairy lights. Dusk did gorgeous things to the streets around us. Outside one house there were around a dozen folding chairs, all lilac, and a cluster of a family standing around, having an audibly lovely time. One boy child holds sparklers out for presumably his cousins and brothers and neighbours, too many of them in his hand and, yeah, for a moment I worried about his fingers, but it is cinematic, their young awe at the brightness of the ignition, the bouquet of grey wire and powder that is less impressive than a dead cluster of flowers until it is set alight. The boy holds stars in his hands and the other kids on the street corner are astounded and so am I.

As we reach the end of the house-forest there is a little, rounded patch of green in the centre of what is almost a cul-de-sac. In the parklet there are rose bushes, many of them, arranged nicely but all dead except for a few surviving blooms. There are small avenues of grass between the flowerbeds, and in the centre a couple of benches. Girl children lie around in the hub of grass at the heart of the dead garden and talk, and laugh, staring up at the bruising sky, waiting for fireworks, waiting for something. One or two sit on the benches and swing their baby-deer legs. Most of their dresses and clothes are white. That's summertime, I guess. I hope they're all OK – the scene is borderline serial-killer looking. Maybe if the roses were in bloom it would be nicer, but there's something dark about so many dead flowers all together and then at the core of their arrangement bright, wide-eyed kids waiting for fireworks, waiting for celebration.

On our way through the city I notice that the American flag is hanging from a crane by the river, suspended by invisible wire. It ripples in the night air and looks almost like it is liquid, suspended in space, stars and stripes forever and ever and ever, levitating over all of us. We hit a karaoke bar in Oldtown. It is empty at first but for us four, and a table at the back of skinny dudes with tattoos and earlobes stretched to the size of quarters. Nate and Amanda are big into karaoke and we've gone drinking and singing with them before in Berkeley. There's something really raw and honest about it, about who people become when they have that mic in their hands; even if they aren't astonishing singers it doesn't matter because up there there's something that comes over you and it isn't even remotely connected to reality – it is something else.

The skinny dudes with tattoos all sing rap songs and throw shapes out into the crowd. Nate belts down 'Ms Jackson', and it is the fifth State he's sang it in and I think this is incredible. CB sits out the singing because all the skinny white dudes singing rap songs make him feel self-conscious about his usual choice ('Intergalactic' by the Beastie Boys). Amanda takes 'Jump in the Line,' which I have never heard done at karaoke before, and I think this is awesome, and at some point an entire bridal shower enters the bar. All skinny, drunk, excited girls. I like them immediately, their enthusiasm, but am also kind of sad because I'm not sure I'll ever get a bridal shower or hen party or anything like that, and if I do I'm not sure when it'll be. They seem to enjoy my brief transformation into Bonnie Tyler, but they become waves of froth and foam at the high tops of one of the skinny white dudes who, before singing 'The Thong Song', asks them if they're going to get white-girl wasted and they scream, yes, yes, they are. Basically everyone in this bar is white, and white people mocking other white people for being white is really strange to me. I think all four of us are a little queasy about it – I realize in this moment that I find the diversity of San Francisco really comforting. The bride sings 'Don't Stop Believin'', and I am really happy for her and her friends – they really mean every lyric they drunkenly chorus, a choir of enthusiasm, of hope.

There are shenanigans with getting back into the apartment. At least that's how the dude whose mom's house it is explains it when we finally get in touch with him, shenanigans, so sorry about all the shenanigans. See, our keys don't work. Our phones are all dead, so none of us can call him. The car is almost out of gas so we can't use the charger in the car. So, we try to find a twenty-four-hour gas station, which (top tip for tourists) doesn't exist in Portland. We stop at a 7-11 and I use my mam voice on the guy behind the counter and he lets us charge our phones. Nate and Amanda stand inside the 7-11 and CB and I smoke cigarettes outside. I tell him I'm totally down with sleeping in the car. He smiles. When one of the phones finally wakes up I call the dude whose mom's house we're staying in. Shenanigans, he says, the last renters must have lost one of the keys and had the wrong one copied — he says he'll be right there. When we return and he lets us in he offers to refund us some of what we paid, so we'll give the place a good review. He's really very sweet, baseball cap, indeterminate late-teens/mid-twenties looking. There are croissants in the refrigerator and cream cheese and bagels. We're so glad to be inside — it's like 2 a.m., God, we're such parents. We smoke in the little decking area for a while and there is a tiny bat, sleeping, hanging on the wooden fire escape above us and it clatters away into the night, unexpected and noisy, and I tell it to piss off. Absolute shenanigans.

The next day we eat brunch somewhere twee, a renovated house that is now a tea room with a vintage clothes shop on the side. It's cheap and good, sort of soul-food breakfast stuff, nothing exciting. Mostly biscuits and things — biscuits being scones here in America as opposed to, like, digestives and Rich Tea and Custard Creams. The coffee, in fact, is almost incredible, and we drink it out of teacups and we talk about it a lot. A girl with glasses and tattoos pulls into the café on a bike at one point and delivers them more coffee in brown packages from the basket of her bike. I am half rolling my eyes and half considering moving here.

We find parking in a lot next to another coffee shop and Nate defeats his dad instincts once again in taking the first place to park instead of the best place to park – but Powell's looms.

Powell's is roughly the size of an airport. It is miles of books, floors and floors of them: the map is colour coded. I touch the books as I pass them in the New Releases section. At this point in time I am almost finished writing my travel story about the year that has just passed, have signed my contract and passed over my first draft, not including this postscript. I touch their covers and think about being a person who makes things up and writes them down and am very moved by the size of this bookstore, the almost archival nature of it, the towering shelves full of people's effort and love and blood and sweat and tears. My heart swells, and I wander off alone for a while to think about finally joining these kinds of shelves, what that means. I buy a couple of zines, one for my sister and one for me, and a book written by a girl my age who writes about sex on the internet and is kind of famous in New York. I think about how I want there to be more girls my age writing about real life. CB and Nate both buy books by this pop-culture critic they really like and they are boyish in their excitement about it.

We leave and stand in line for Voodoo Donuts. It is a tiny corner bakery, painted bright pink, open twenty-four hours, with such concoctions on its menu as the Triple Chocolate Penetration Donut (chocolate cake, chocolate frosting, topped with Cocoa Puffs), the Diablos Rex (chocolate cake, chocolate frosting, vanilla pentagram drawn on top with red sprinkles and chocolate chips in the hole) and the Bacon Maple Bar (maple frosting? Bacon on top? I know, right?) The list is almost endless. The line, also, is almost endless, but we say, fuck it, we've queued for worse in San Francisco, and set up camp with our new books. Amanda reads one of the zines and I am cautious about how graphic the essay about sex-work I am reading is so I try to lean away from the teenage girls standing behind us. Nate and CB read their books. None of us looks at our phones. The sun is really intense and the line moves along steadily. The smell of the bakery is heady once we get closer to the building.

I notice that beside the bakery there's an old-fashioned-looking little cinema, which has a sign up on the listings board over the door that shows a cartoon image of a girl that is also kind of a cat wearing a maid's uniform. The cinema shows Japanese animated pornography on the weekends. I think this is brilliant and hilarious. We talk about writing as we stand in the line, about how it's kind of sad that people in their twenties are expected to relate to the work of writers who grew up at an entirely different time to us. Nate says, 'Fucking baby boomers' – and the white-haired couple in front of us are slightly uncomfortable, but we figure it's about time. I feel way better about what I chose to do with my life by the time we hit the door and finally break into the cool, delicious air of Voodoo. We panic in the face of the endless menu. Sriracha basil donuts? Rapper's Delight (maple, spliff-looking, cream centered thing)? Captain My Captain (heavily involves Cap'n Crunch cereal)? 'Look,' CB says, 'just give us two of the Voodoo Dozen.'

We leave carrying two enormous pink boxes, which contain twenty-four donuts, some of which are the size of my face. We head back to the car for the journey home. It is coming up on late afternoon – we'll have to stop someplace tonight. We say, hey, why not Ashland – a small, nowhere town with a pretty famous Shakespeare festival around five hours from here. We say, hey, why not, see how we go. We'd stopped there for coffee in a terrifying diner called the Wild Goose on the way up; we figure we can revisit, like our drive home tomorrow will be achievable if we crash there. Six hours and six hours: that's normal, that's doable.

There is a strip club on the highway that has an all-you-can-eat buffet that opens at three in the afternoon. Great arcs of water spray the crops in the fields we pass like white fireworks. Sometimes they spiral, like the outstretched arms of a dancing child.

I realize that we forgot the socks for my sister. That's OK though. At this moment she is in London on her first trip abroad with her friends, just done with school forever, just having everything change. I feel very close to her, even though we're very far apart. I hope she's doing OK, but I know in my heart she definitely is. The tape deck starts to die on us. Weird thing, the tape deck – obsolete but benevolent, some cheerful musical zombie letting us use its helpless corpse to summon voices from a time when it was useful. More nineties hits carry us into the night, angelic.

In the last Oregon sun we're going to see, something starts to refract light around the car. 'Nate,' Amanda says, 'you have fairies all over you – where are they coming from?' We fumble around, assuming it's a glass surface on one of our phones, but the tiny rainbows are everywhere. It's kind of gorgeous, and Amanda realizes suddenly that it's from the long pendant she's wearing around her neck.

Five hours happen. I don't know how they happen but they do. Putting the country underfoot is effortless. We accidentally turn off the freeway down a winding lane at one point where there are shacks and probably guns. We make it out alive. We stop at a giant trucker Mecca. It gets dark. I am sitting in the front, slightly stupid from anti-nauseants again, and the sky turns so black and the stars turn so white. I don't think I've ever seen them like this before and am transfixed. Space Mountain has nothing on this, this kaleidoscope, this infinity.

We eat in the Wild Goose again and the air conditioning is baltic. The waitress has a bouffant and a drawl – she's very polite but straight out of a movie. There is karaoke in the bar in the back, and we are calling every hotel in Ashland to find somewhere to stay. This is a whole world of no. No rooms. We call thirteen hotels and it is, like, eleven at night and we're starting to get convinced we're sleeping in the car. The nearest free motel is in a town near the border called Weed. We laugh for ages at this, delirious from the road. We rent the fifty-dollar room and we drive into the night towards it. A town called Weed. For fuck's sake.

In the redwoods we pass a great crucifix illuminated on the grassy roadside. It is made cleanly but without circumstance, like two neat floorboards nailed together. There are stadium-strength floodlights at its base, and it shines with an unearned grandeur, just two sticks stuck together. At its base, a sign rests. FORGIVE THEM, it says. I don't stop thinking about that for a while.

When we get into our tiny room in the tiny old motel, we laugh for a while at how awful it is. A town called

Weed, an extended truck stop, somewhere time-locked and surreal. There's the Weed Chamber of Commerce. The Weed Store! The Weed Diner! The town slogan is 'Weed like to Welcome You!' There is an unstoppable pull of laughter, a hysteria, and I put my face in my hands and don't realize I haven't laughed in this way in a long time. Even when I think I'm OK, that laughter is just not something that happens in America. Maybe it hadn't even happened in Ireland for a long time either. There are tears rolling down my cheeks, and my jaw does that weird clicky thing; I cannot breathe because I am laughing so hard, Amanda and Nate and Ceri all laughing so hard.

We recover and sleep. Before the light goes off I see a black insect the size of a teacup scuttle up past the mirror and into the air conditioner. My stomach lurches and I wrap myself in my Super Mario blanket (I've had it for a long time and it comes to most overnight places with me, especially hotels that are potentially gross). I am not able to sleep because the room is so old, our knots of hilarity faded now as one by one snores lift from the boys' bodies and the night begins to thicken, rolling later and later. I begin to get extremely uncomfortable in the room. I half-dream my boat dream and wake up with a pressure in my back. I feel like someone has died in this room and I can't get that out of my head. There is a sinisterness that grows and grows as the night rolls in and I can't sleep, not at all. FORGIVE THEM, the crucifix says.

Morning turns up with a sequence of flat, tuneless 'Om' from the room above us. Yoga chanting usually sounds like peace to me, but this is a reverberating drone, intentionally loud, inflected all wrong. It wakes the other three one by one and I lie around with my eyes closed while they rise. We eat in the Weed Diner and I manage to control myself and do not steal the mug that says 'Weed Like To Welcome You'.

We hit the road again, and California shows up all suddenly – I'd never realized why they call it the Golden State before. The hills that greet us as we get nearer the bay are triangular, almost pyramids, covered in short, rough, golden grass. They are like the shoulder blades of a crouching lion, angular and regal. By the time we hit the Oakland traffic, heavy because of an evening Giants' game, we are blaring Britney Spears from the windows and singing. We sit stock still in a grid of cars and are undefeated by this slow crawl back into the Bay, its arms crossed, as though saying, well, what do you think you were doing running off to Oregon like that? Like a stern mother standing at the hall door at seven in the morning when you were due home at midnight, the Bay will let us in, because she has to, because we're part of her vast, weird family, but slowly, almost reluctantly.

Let me tell you about the opposite of being lost. The opposite of being lost is being found. Let me tell you about leaving everything you had in a tender city for an empty apartment in a strange city you know nothing about only hills, bridges and Harvey Milk. Let me tell you, as we crawl back through the Bay after a four-day road trip all our walls are down, all the stupid music chosen and aired proudly in the little white minivan – I guess we didn't say much about our lives, our real lives, to each other, but I'm not sure that was even necessary. This feels like being found. This feels like everything has stopped, at last, being about lostness, but is instead about finding things on the way. Gone doesn't sound like a sad word any more. Neither does lost. Lost is an exclamation point here, right here on the map, where the red dotted line across the world, across adulthood, across adventure, finally begins.